Eyes, Ears, and Daggers

Eyes, Ears, and Daggers is arguably the best book on the relationship of the modern Central Intelligence Agency (CIA) and the Special Operations Forces (SOF). From the American Revolution to the Office of Strategic Services and the subsequent birth of the CIA and the SOF, the relationship among intelligence, paramilitary, psychological operations, the SOF, and the broader Special Operations community can be summed up as yin and yang, constantly adjusting, rebalancing, and ebbing and flowing with the good and the bad. When it has counted, the CIA's resources, relationships, and authorities, combined with the SOF capabilities and capacity, have provided our nation with exquisite tactical actions that have achieved decisive and often strategic effects. Thomas Henriksen's well-researched work, using analyses based on open-source and published works, will serve students, researchers, and the public, providing an understanding of the unique and incredible relationship between two of our nation's most important organizations: the CIA and the SOF.

David S. Maxwell *(colonel, ret., US Army Special Forces),*
associate director, Center for Security Studies, Georgetown University

This clearly written account of the evolution of the working relationship between irregular US military units and the paramilitary activities of the Central Intelligence Agency (CIA) is exciting and important. Henriksen's compelling analysis is that cooperation between Special Operation Forces and the CIA is necessary in today's struggle against the large terrorist organizations, Al Qaeda and ISIS, that are operating in many countries of the Islamic world.

John Deutch, *former director of the Central Intelligence Agency*
and deputy secretary of defense

Eyes, Ears, and Daggers is a primer on what makes our Special Operations Forces so special. Henriksen shows how the Central Intelligence Agency's (CIA's) inability to provide the intelligence essential to the military forces' operation has caused the Pentagon to develop its own intelligence, how the CIA pushed back, and how battlefield necessity has been key to mastering bureaucratic rivalries. This book teaches the cautionary lesson that the skills and bravery of frontline operators are hostage to high officials' proper focus on the mission to be accomplished. It should be read by all who count on our special forces in the fight against terrorism.

Angelo Codevilla, *professor emeritus of*
international relations at Boston University

Eyes,
Ears &
Daggers

Eyes, Ears & Daggers

Special Operations Forces and the Central Intelligence Agency in America's Evolving Struggle against Terrorism

Thomas H. Henriksen

HOOVER INSTITUTION PRESS

Stanford University   Stanford, California

www.hoover.org

Hoover Institution Press Publication No. 671

Hoover Institution at Leland Stanford Junior University,
Stanford, California 94305-6003

First printing 2016
23 22 21 20 19 18 17 16   8 7 6 5 4 3 2 1

Manufactured in the United States of America

The paper used in this publication meets the minimum Requirements of the American National Standard for Information Sciences—Permanence of Paper for Printed Library Materials, ANSI/NISO Z39.48-1992. ♾

Library of Congress Cataloging-in-Publication Data
Names: Henriksen, Thomas H., author.
Title: Eyes, ears, and daggers : special operations forces and the Central
   Intelligence Agency in America's evolving struggle against terrorism /
   Thomas H. Henriksen.
Other titles: Hoover Institution Press publication ; 671.
Description: Stanford, CA : Hoover Institution Press, 2016. | Series: Hoover
   Institution Press publication ; no. 671
Identifiers: LCCN 2016023703 (print) | LCCN 2016024284 (ebook) |
   ISBN 9780817919740 (clothbound : alk. paper) | ISBN 9780817919764 (EPUB) |
   ISBN 9780817919771 (Mobipocket) | ISBN 9780817919788 (EPDF) |
Subjects: LCSH: Terrorism—United States—Prevention—History. |
   Terrorism—Government policy—United States—History. | Special forces
   (Military science)—United States—History. | United States. Central
   Intelligence Agency—History. | Interagency coordination—United
   States—History.
Classification: LCC HV6432.H475 2016 (print) | LCC HV6432 (ebook) |
   DDC 363.325/170973—dc23
LC record available at https://lccn.loc.gov/2016023703

For Jim Harrison, onetime classmate and enduring friend,
who lived part of the story of this book in the Vietnam War.

Contents

Acknowledgments

I T IS OFTEN SAID that most institutions are unique in their own way. The Hoover Institution is more unique than most. Not only does it provide all manner of administrative and technical support to its fellows but its legendary standing also brings together an array of high-profile former government officials, eminent resident fellows, and renowned visiting scholars who intellectually stimulate and contribute to the research and writing conducted under its auspices. Its director, Thomas Gilligan, and his associates enable the institution's researchers to concentrate on scholarship, free of many of the time-consuming administrative constraints that can hinder and limit investigation and thought. Once more, I am indebted to my colleagues for their commentary and exchanges.

Over the course of researching and writing this volume, I have been blessed by many first-rate research assistants, who helped in all aspects of its creation. They are Nicholas Siekierski, Alexander Fulbright, Lisa Teruel, Gabriel Shapiro, and Jeanene Harlick. Each made distinct contributions to the book. The errors, of course, remain my own despite their assistance.

Nothing would have been read or written without the deep encouragement and loving support of my wife, Margaret Mary, and our family—Heather, Damien, Liv, and Lucy. They deserve much more than a perfunctory thank you from an author. Indeed, they made this book and the others possible.

Acronyms and Abbreviations

AMISOM	African Union Mission in Somalia
AQAP	al Qaeda in the Arabian Peninsula
AQI	al Qaeda in Iraq
ASD/SOLIC	Assistant Secretary of Defense for Special Operations/Low-Intensity Conflict
CENTCOM	U.S. Central Command
CIA	Central Intelligence Agency
CIDG	Civilian Irregular Defense Group
COI	Coordinator of Information
CRT	Crisis response team
CTC	Counterterrorism Center
CTPT	Counterterrorism Pursuit Team
CTS	Counterterrorism Service (Iraq)
DIA	Defense Intelligence Agency
EKIA	Enemy Killed in Action
IRA	Irish Republican Army
ISA	Intelligence Support Activity
ISAF	International Security Assistance Force
ISIS	Islamic State of Iraq and Syria
JCS	Joint Chiefs of Staff
JIATF	Joint Interagency Task Force
JSOC	Joint Special Operations Command

JSOTF-NCR	Joint Special Operations Task Force—National Capital Region
MACV	Military Assistance Command Vietnam
NSA	National Security Agency
NSC	National Security Council
OCPW	Office of the Chief of Psychological Warfare
ONI	Office of Naval Intelligence
OSS	Office of Strategic Services
SACSA	Special Assistant for Counterinsurgency and Special Activities
SAD	Special Activities Division
SMU	Special Mission Units
SOE	Special Operations Executive
SOF	Special Operations Forces
SOG	Studies and Observation Group
USSOCOM	U.S. Special Operations Command
VC	Viet Cong

chapter one

America's Early Unconventional Ventures

Each war tells us something about the way the next war will be
fought.

Herodotus

One of the things we have seen since 9/11 is an extraordinary
coming together, particularly the CIA and the military, in working together and fusing intelligence and operations in a way that
just, I think, is unique in anybody's history.

Robert Gates[1]

WHEN NATHAN HALE stood on the scaffold in 1776 and uttered his
immortal regret that he had only one life to give for his
country, he came to embody a timeless patriot. In retrospect,
Hale was also a progenitor of the soldier-spy fusion that has
become so noteworthy in the early twenty-first-century conflict
with jihadi terrorism. Days before his execution, the young military officer had volunteered to dress in civilian clothes, go
behind enemy lines, and scout out the Red Coats' plans at the
start of the American Revolution. His fellow officers shrank
from the mission out of fear of dying from an ignominious execution by hanging, rather than an ennobling death on the battle-

field. The British caught and hanged the twenty-one-year-old captain from the Seventh Connecticut regiment for spying. Captain Hale's secret mission is significant for its present-day relevance as well as its patriotism. His intelligence gathering inside British-occupied New York City blurred the lines separating soldier and spy. It was an early version of "sheep dipping," the contemporary practice of informal reidentification in which soldiers become spies. More than two centuries after the Yale-educated schoolteacher's death, America's counterterrorism campaign underwent a similar obscuring over the roles between elite warriors and intelligence officials in the antiterrorism battle. This military-intelligence overlap was not foreordained. Quite the contrary, the two communities—military and intelligence—were often at odds throughout their histories. Their contemporary blending, indeed, might just be a temporary realignment. A return to their traditional rivalry is not out of the question.

Both the Special Operations Forces (SOF) and the Central Intelligence Agency (CIA) are of relatively recent formation. Their antecedents, nonetheless, stretch back further than the immediate post–World War II era, which marked the creation of both entities. Irregular armed forces have been a part of America's military traditions from as early as the Revolutionary War up to the current battle against violent Islamist extremism in the Middle East, Africa, and other parts of the world. Spying enjoys a less-rich tradition in America's past, although it, too, underwent a quantum leap during the Cold War.

Both communities—special warriors and intelligence officers—have served as the nation's eyes, ears, and daggers, often in close cooperation, but occasionally at cross-purposes, as this account traces and analyzes. Yet in bureaucratic tug-of-wars, neither the Special Operations Forces nor the Central Intelligence Agency has been each other's main antagonist. Rather, they have clashed with their closest competitor. For SOF, this has meant turf battles with the regular military forces. For the CIA, it has meant bureaucratic tussles chiefly with the State Department and the Federal Bureau of Investigation (FBI), not the Pentagon. The SOF-CIA partnership grew to become a highly effective weapon against jihadi terrorists bent on murdering or converting other populations to their twisted version of Islam. The September 11, 2001, terrorist attack, in fact, heralded a new era for the two secretive security arms of the U.S. government, an era that is the subject of this anatomy.

The attack on the Twin Towers shelved America's Cold War thinking about security. By adopting an intelligence-driven, targeted counterstrike weapon against terrorists, the United States went from a Cold War Goliath to a lithe and nimble bearer of a deadly sling, thanks in no small measure to the SOF and CIA contribution. Much of the reorientation developed from the close SOF-CIA linkage, as is well known to both communities. The purpose of this narrative is to sketch very briefly the warrior-spy connection before and then more fully after the formation of the Special Operations Forces and the Central Intelligence Agency. Even a "wave-top" skimming of this complex interaction suggests that their history is notable for instances of cooperating, competing, circumventing, and even cutting each other out of the action. By revisiting and appreciating their respective histories prior to their partnering to combat Islamist terrorism, the author hopes to provide a clearer understanding of their interaction and offer lessons for the future.

Spying, Binoculars, and Telegraph Cables

Students of America's cloak-and-dagger operations have a nodding acquaintance with espionage that dates to the country's war of independence from Britain. Nathan Hale's behind-the-lines spying inaugurated the fledgling nation's quest for intelligence about its powerful foe. In another league from Hale's snooping was a renowned spymaster, string-pulling his agents for information. George Washington not only stood first in the hearts of his countrymen but also ranked first among the Founding Fathers in his fascination with and reliance on espionage. Young Washington learned firsthand the importance of intelligence during the French and Indian War (1754–63), when he served under British general Edward Braddock, whose defeat and death at Fort Duquesne (now Pittsburgh) stemmed, in part, from ignorance about his enemy's forces.

When Washington assumed command of the Continental army, he resolved to obtain intelligence about his British opponent by every means. Spies were dispatched to learn British movements and designs. Worried about English spies and American sympathizers with the Crown, he took measures to prevent them from conveying information to the British about the Continental army's maneuvers and activities. The Continental Congress also grasped the importance of foreign intelligence. It established the Committee of Secret Correspondence, which one contemporary historian characterized as "the distant ancestor of today's CIA."[2] The group corresponded with American well-wishers who lived in Europe so as to gain intelligence about the European governments' predisposition toward the American Revolution. General Washington was naturally far more interested in military information.

So while Nathan Hale won enduring fame, Washington commanded a constellation of spies who proved much more successful than the young Connecticut officer. This eyes-and-ears network also performed counterespionage, detecting the treason of Benedict Arnold—the infamous American turncoat who switched to George III's side. General Washington also utilized agents to spread bogus information about his army's strength and intentions. He even deceived British generals about his strategy until the trap was sprung, leading to the surrender of Lord Cornwallis at Yorktown and the American defeat of Great Britain.

As the first president of the new Republic, George Washington retained his interest in things clandestine. His secret service fund, a line item in the nation's budget, grew to nearly 12 percent, or about $1 million, by his third year in office. President Washington disbursed these monies for bribing foreign officials and even ransoming sailors held by the Barbary pirates. These predators operated out of North African city-states and preyed on American merchant ships. Despite the contemporary view of late-eighteenth-century gentility, Congress understood the necessity of covert measures; it cut the nation's first commander-in-chief considerable slack in espionage endeavors. Congress merely required the president to certify the amounts expended but permitted him to conceal the purpose and recipients. These and related operations foreshadowed those practiced after the Central Intelligence Act of 1949.[3]

George Washington's role as spymaster notwithstanding, his successors did not follow his pioneering role. If anything, they allowed the U.S. intelligence capacity to atrophy with dire consequences. America's dismal intelligence service contributed to the lack of adequate defense for the White House, which the British burned during the War of 1812. President James Madison barely escaped the capital in advance of Britain's capture and torching of his residence. Behind their Atlantic moat, Americans seemed oblivious to the importance of intelligence about their potential adversaries. Even during the Mexican War (1846–48), the commanding officer, General Zachary Taylor, obtained his knowledge of the Mexican army through his binoculars. His deputy,

Winfield Scott, did gain approval from President James Polk to set up the Mexican Spy Company, which relied on the outlaw Manuel Dominguez and his bandit followers to hand over military intelligence about Mexican defenses. It was not the last time that U.S. presidents and their military officers paid off less-than-savory agents to spy.

The Civil War (1861–65) marked a period of mostly amateurish spying by both sides. In fact, Northern and Southern military officers and civilian officials regularly scoured each other's newspapers to glean information about their foes. Then, as now, the press's war coverage revealed actionable intelligence. Journalists published details on the troop strength, location, and destination of military units. This breach of security concerned both sides. Washington and Richmond tried to shut down the newspapers. Political leaders did hire spies to collect information on their enemies. Field commanders likewise set up their own intelligence operations to do reconnaissance on their adversaries and to limit knowledge of their respective forces. The history of Union and Confederate espionage, with its passions and bumbling, is ably told by Alan Axelrod in *The War between the Spies*. But as Axelrod acknowledged, the spies were amateurs, "usually ordinary soldiers and civilians who, on one or more occasions, did some spying."[4] His account overflowed with assassins, conspirators, and secret service forerunners—all part of present-day intelligence and covert operations.

After the Civil War, investments in spies, espionage, and covert operators dwindled through the end of the nineteenth century. Some noteworthy departments were established, however. The Secret Service came into existence in 1865, first as an agency to investigate forgeries in the new paper currency that had appeared three years earlier. After the Secret Service uncovered a plot in 1894 to assassinate President Glover Cleveland, it assumed the mission of safeguarding the president, the vice president, and their families, as well as the integrity of the American currency. Its dual missions became permanent after the assassination of President William McKinley in 1901.

In the course of the 1880s, both the U.S. Navy and U.S. Army established intelligence departments. The Office of Naval Intelligence (ONI) collected information about foreign navies that might be useful in time of war. Likewise, the Military Intelligence Division, staffed initially by one officer, gathered material on foreign armies of possible use to the War Department and the Army. For the U.S. Navy, the ONI played a pivotal role in the extraordinary naval expansion at the dawn of the twentieth century. Theodore Roosevelt, as assistant secretary of the Navy (well before his presidency), capitalized on ONI reports to push for a giant shipbuilding program that saw the Navy's blue-water fleet mushroom in capital ships.[5] As president, Roosevelt was not averse to using underhanded measures to accomplish his goals abroad.

Covert action, in fact, played a hand in the White House's acquisition of the Panama Canal Zone. Unmistakable U.S. sympathy for the Panamanian insurrectionists encouraged them to revolt against their Colombian rulers in 1903. Next, Washington ran interference for the rebels. The Colombian commander of the offshore fleet was bribed to sail away without shelling the Panamanians. The U.S. Navy also blocked Colombia's ships from landing reinforcements to reestablish its rule. The United States formally recognized the Republic of Panama in 1904, leased the ten-mile strip on each side of the proposed waterway, and resumed construction of the transoceanic canal, which was completed in 1914.

During World War I, U.S. intelligence efforts foiled Germany's operations to influence American public opinion against Great

Britain. German agents tried to shift U.S. sentiment toward Germany and away from Britain. Along with planting pro-German articles in American newspapers, the Kaiser's agents blew up two large munitions factories in New Jersey. Despite Berlin's sabotage and media manipulations, which often backfired against Germany, Washington lacked a specialized espionage department. As a defense, President Woodrow Wilson ordered the Secret Service to investigate German businessmen paying subsidies to German-American organizations. The U.S. Justice Department, moreover, linked the German embassy with subversive actions.[6]

The Army and Navy beefed up their military intelligence proficiency during the war. Each branch employed more than a thousand personnel by the armistice signing in 1918. A prominent innovation during the war was the first signals intelligence office, whose focus was on preventing domestic subversion. The signals intelligence specialists deciphered encrypted messages and handed over evidence to the Bureau of Investigation, the forerunner of the FBI. All the fledgling counterespionage departments were very busy because of the large number of German immigrants living within the United States.

Once at war against Imperial Germany and its allies in 1917, the Wilson administration engaged in a covert operation with Britain to persuade Russia to remain in the war after its February Revolution, which overthrew the tsar in early 1917. Washington spent modest sums of money to place pro-war newspaper articles in the Russian press. London took an even more extravagant approach by wining and dining Russian government officials. Still, Washington's modest contribution to persuading the Russian Provisional Government to stay in the fight against the Central Powers came to naught. By mid-1917, the Russian army collapsed as a fighting force after repeated defeats at the hands of the German forces and their Austro-Hungarian allies. Moscow's contribution to the Allied cause ended when Vladimir Lenin's Bolsheviks tossed out the provisional government in the October Revolution. Soviet Russia's new rulers soon broke ranks with the Allies and concluded a separate peace with Berlin in order to concentrate on consolidating their power amid the ensuing civil war, which engulfed much of the country. The capitalist West had no sway with Communist Russia. After Lenin settled for a harsh peace with the Central Powers, the Allies slugged it out with Germany, now freed from the two-front war.

As expected, the end of the war brought a hasty return to business as usual for the United States. It made severe reductions in the nation's military and intelligence capabilities. The federal government quickly slashed funding for intelligence as well as demobilized its armed forces. Unlike other major powers, America still lacked a specialized foreign espionage organization at the close of the war. The war had recorded a temporary boost in manpower and effectiveness of army and naval intelligence, but peace scuttled that progress. Nor were the 1920s and early 1930s the propitious environments for setting up overseas spy operations. President Wilson subscribed to a brave new world of open diplomacy openly arrived at, departing from what the old powers of Europe did behind closed doors. Moreover, America looked inward as isolationist sentiments took hold among political elites and ordinary people alike. American naiveté about the outside world came into sharp relief when Henry L. Stimson (Herbert Hoover's secretary of state and Franklin Roosevelt's secretary of war) averred that "gentlemen don't read each other's mail."[7]

That said, the United States did score an intelligence coup during the first year of the incoming Warren Harding administration. At the Washington Conference on the Limitations of Armaments in 1921, Americans decrypted Japanese telegraph cables from Tokyo. Knowledge of Japan's real diplomatic bargaining position enabled Washington to stand firm on Japanese demands to exceed the 10:6 naval ratio of capital ships with the United States.[8] The U.S. position prevailed. The Japanese, whose real threshold was revealed in the decoded message, accepted the lower ratio. American intelligence breakthroughs, however, were all too rare in the interwar period, as the attack on Pearl Harbor attested. But they were not unprecedented once the Pacific war started. The American proficiency in cracking the wartime Japanese codes enabled Washington to learn of Tokyo's plans for the conquest of Midway Island. The astounding U.S. naval victory over the Imperial fleet was, in part, made possible by foreknowledge of Japan's strategy. America's signals intelligence came of age during the Pacific war.

Protected by two vast oceans, the United States progressed through the first 170 years of its history without a meaningful national intelligence enterprise. The American embrace of the Marquess of Queensberry rules for collecting intelligence lingered into the twentieth century before the gloves finally came off. It was World War II and the Cold War aftermath that revolutionized American attitudes.[9] Before considering the extraordinary transformation that the 1941–45 war brought to American intelligence resources, however, it is appropriate to shift attention to the other pillar of the contemporary SOF-CIA alignment—the irregular warfare tradition.

Irregular Warfare as an American Tradition

Unlike spying, America's irregular warfare tradition enjoys a deeper cultural heritage. Its lineage stretches back to at least the French and Indian War, when regular soldiers embraced the tactics of Native American warriors. Rather than following the parade-ground drills of troops marching into battle, the Native American tribesmen resorted to ambushes, small-unit attacks, and firing from behind trees to catch their adversaries off guard. Both French and American soldiers observed, adopted, and put into practice this hit-and-run warfare.

When the American Revolution broke out, the colonists relied on different tactics. George Washington fought a largely conventional conflict along European lines. But as every schoolchild knows, other American forces fired from behind cover as they fell back when confronted with superior Red Coat formations. Some legendary local commanders emerged. Francis Marion, the "Swamp Fox," disrupted British control of the Carolinas with surprise attacks and unexpected maneuvers. Ethan Allen and his Green Mountain Boys kept the Red Coats off balance with hit-and-run assaults in New England. These unconventional leaders waged an insurgency against an army of occupation that demanded loyalty to the Crown and payment to George III's treasury.

Decades later, the American Civil War witnessed a host of irregular warfare practitioners on both sides of the four-year conflict. These fighters operated behind the lines of the conventional infantry and cavalry forces. The renegades raided, disrupted governance, and tied down disproportionate numbers of regular forces who strove to kill or capture their tormentors. John Mosby and his Mosby's Rangers, as well as Nathan Bedford Forrest and his raiders, carved out bloody reputations as effective tacticians of guerrilla warfare in the cause of the Confederate States. From the Union's regular army came such scorched-earth commanders as Philip Sheridan, who pillaged and burned the Shenandoah Valley, and William Tecumseh Sherman, who laid waste to the Deep South in his infamous March to the Sea.

After the Civil War, the U.S. Army turned its attention back toward the untamed forests and plains in the West to secure a continental passage to California. Irregular-fighting tactics played a prominent role in the westward conquest of the American continent until near the end of the nineteenth century. Conflicts raged against the indigenous inhabitants as land-seeking settlers streamed from the Eastern Seaboard to the interior plains. Most engagements were small-unit actions in which the U.S. Army borrowed American Indian tactics of stealth, surprise, and ambush. Not all the engagements ended in a U.S. victory. General George Custer's defeat at the Little Bighorn, a loss born of hubris, poor planning, and tactical errors, has served as a cautionary lesson for students of war ever since 1876.

The conclusion of the so-called Indian Wars marked the eclipse of the irregular-fighting capacity among U.S. military forces for nearly a quarter of a century. The American traditions of frontier warfare and inherent Yankee ingenuity, however, are traits that must not be dismissed without brief reference. These frontier soldiers possessed the qualities of stealth, surprise, and self-reliance that later generations of Special Operations Forces would draw on and incorporate into the present-day antiterrorism campaign and counterinsurgency operations.

Not until the Spanish-American War would U.S. ground forces wage a modern-day counterinsurgency against guerrillas. The Philippine War (1899–1902) found the United States on the receiving end of an insurgency fought by a determined band of Filipinos for the right of independence against colonial-type rule from Washington. Ultimately, the United States prevailed in its counterinsurgency campaign by a mixture of innovative techniques and military competency.[10] Afterward, the U.S. military occupied Haiti in an operation that turned into an early version of nation building on the impoverished island. The Marine Corps soon found itself embroiled in a string of small conflicts in Cuba, Honduras, Nicaragua, and the Dominican Republic. Marines wrote of their experiences in the "Banana Wars" in a series of articles, which were distilled into their encyclopedic *Small Wars Manual* in 1940, a classic handbook for security operations in underdeveloped lands.[11]

The lessons learned from the Philippines and Caribbean interventions were overshadowed by the mammoth conventional world wars of the twentieth century. World War I's trench warfare swept away the lingering familiarity with irregular fighting. Counterinsurgency proficiency no longer seemed relevant with the introduction of biplanes, tanks, and massed infantry charges across no-man's-lands in the teeth of machine gun fire. The toll in lives was so steep that the war did seem to be a harbinger of lasting peace. After all, the war had been fought to end wars. Immediately following World War I, the United States demobilized its land forces and looked inward to the Roaring Twenties and then the Great Depression. In a short time, though, hypernationalism, rampant militarism, and wicked ideologies stalked the European and Asian landscapes, drawing America into a second world conflagration. This time, however, the events during World War II prompted some American leaders to turn to irregular warfare tactics.

chapter two

World War II and After:
The Catalysts for Cloak and Dagger

THE COMBATANTS in the global conflict that was World War II forged vast regular armies, navies, and air fleets, which battled steel on steel across the planet's plains, seas, and skies. Yet the paradox of World War II lies in the fact that the titanic conventional Armageddon planted the seeds for a far different form of warfare. While its origins were ancient, this irregular warfare and its reliance on guerrilla tactics, stealth, and sabotage struck most military officers of the 1940s as little more than a diversion from the classic force-on-force battles raging around the globe. Three-quarters of a century later—when a terrorist attack perpetrated by radical Islamists hit defenseless targets within the United States—America's military and civilian bureaucracies realized the value of small, versatile, and specially trained units to combat shadowy terrorists. To counter the stateless jihadi networks fixated on transforming countries into an Islamist millennium, the United States turned to special operators and intelligence communities.

A campaign against elusive extremists, who relied on terrorism, demanded a less costly and more finely calibrated weapon than the regular armed forces. This new, whetted instrument relied on specially trained operators and paramilitarized intelligence officers to carry out pinpoint strikes against the nation's adversaries. Their formerly subordinate role in major conventional wars was transformed by the second decade of the twenty-first century as the fight against global jihadis loomed ever larger. This evolution from off-Broadway show to spectacular made-for-Hollywood production was protracted, circuitous, and often delayed by internal opponents from its World War II birth.

The story of special mission units and paramilitary intelligence personnel coming together is fascinating and yet not widely known to the general public. It dates from the darkest days of World War II, when the Third Reich looked invincible. The impetus for specialized fighters and behind-the-lines saboteurs sprang from Britain's setbacks on the European continent after the fall of France to Nazi armies in 1940. Faced with a German occupation of Europe and even a Nazi invasion of the British Isles, the new prime minister, Winston Churchill, turned to cloak-and-dagger tactics to disrupt Berlin's plans. As the Battle of Britain raged in the skies overhead, the Churchill government established the Special Operations Executive (SOE) in 1940 to conduct disruptive sabotage campaigns throughout Axis-ruled Europe.

The SOE deliberately lifted a page from the Irish Republican Army (IRA), which had pursued a guerrilla war for Ireland's independence after World War I. This small-scale but bloody and vengeful insurgency attracts little study from today's counterinsurgency students. Yet it deserves serious attention because contemporary revolutionaries in Russia, China, and elsewhere studied and learned from it. As writer Tony Geraghty pointed out, "The success of the IRA encouraged and taught such diverse anti-colonial movements as the Korean opposition to Japanese occupation, the Burmese nationalists, Indian patriots, and the Bengali New Violence Party."[1] World War II British officials and military officers certainly did not forget the Irish campaign. Winston Churchill himself knew Irish politics intimately from a stint as secretary of state for the Home Office (i.e., the interior department) before World War I. At the tail end of the war and immediately afterward, he served as secretary of state for the army and air force, from which he initiated and oversaw the deployment of the infamous Black and Tans (named for their uniform colors) against Irish rebels. Britain filled the ranks of these auxiliary units (officially known as the Royal Irish Constabulary Reserve Force) with ex-servicemen who often shot prisoners or bystanders and tortured suspected IRA gunmen for information. London's punitive tactics backfired, as the Irish people rallied to the IRA cause against British rule.[2]

The British government lost the fight, and by 1921 most of Ireland broke free from eight centuries of English rule. Only six Protestant counties, making up Ulster in the north, remained loyal to the Union Jack. To its south, predominately Catholic Ireland attained its independence, and in 1948 the Republic of Ireland won its total freedom over five-sixths of the island. The Ulster counties in the north stayed aligned with the United Kingdom. Starting in the 1960s, the Catholic minority in Ulster agitated to join their brethren in greater Ireland. A low-grade urban insurgency ensued, which the British forces managed to keep the lid on for three decades.[3] But the successful independence revolt of the 1920s heavily influenced British planning early in World War II.

The experience of Churchill and his generation in fighting a dirty war in Ireland informed their strategies against the Nazi Reich's occupation of the Continent. The drafter of what was looked on as the founding charter of the SOE was none other than Neville Chamberlain. Newly installed as Britain's wartime leader, Churchill assigned the task of writing the statement for

an organization to sow sabotage and subversion against its continental enemy to Chamberlain after his being sacked as prime
minister in May 1940. In a historical irony, Chamberlain, the
man responsible for the Munich appeasement of Hitler, wrote
the document establishing a cloak-and-dagger organization to
subvert the Hitlerian empire as well as christening the entity as
the Special Operations Executive. The fledgling SOE borrowed
liberally from IRA practices.[4] Their hit-and-run tactics served as
a model for Britain and its European partners to strike at Axis
forces, supply depots, railways, and harbors, all the while garner-
ing intelligence and peddling propaganda. These SOE activities
bred a variety of specialists and units: field operatives, saboteurs,
communication experts, and resistance organizers.[5] And, in turn,
the SOE served as a model to a select few Americans who recognized the usefulness of less-than-conventional approaches to
warfare.

Long before the United States entered the war following the
Pearl Harbor attack, a handful of American officials took note
of Britain's unconventional military steps as an offshoot of its
traditional spying apparatus. British intelligence dates from the
sixteenth-century reign of Elizabeth I. The intervening half of
a millennium afforded the Crown's ministers ample time to
evolve a far-flung and sophisticated intelligence branch that
gained abundant espionage experience on the Continent and
elsewhere.

Faced with Berlin's mastery of the Continent, London fell back
on subversion, sabotage, and espionage to "set Europe ablaze"—
in Churchill's historic characterization.[6] The British government
lacked the conventional wherewithal to breach the German continental defenses. So it opted for an unorthodox war in hopes of
throwing the Reich occupation off balance while restoring hope
of eventual deliverance among the vanquished populations.

By contrast, Britain's American cousins may have been unschooled, but they were fast learners, as their Office of Strategic Services (OSS) demonstrated soon enough. The United States lacked anything comparable to Britain's mid-twentieth-century spy network. The Pearl Harbor calamity awoke the United States to the folly of living without an intelligence service to alert the nation ahead of impending attacks. White House emissaries traveled to Britain following the fall of France to the German army. There they observed not solely the country's intelligence capacity to collect and analyze information but also its intelligence branch's capability to strike the German military, keeping it off balance.[7]

The American observers soaked up abundant details about Britain's unconventional units and irregular warfare techniques. They set about modeling specialized battalions along British service lines. The British Security Coordination, an intelligence network headquartered for a time in New York City, ran espionage operations and conducted guerrilla warfare against German targets. Cooperation between the British Security Coordination and the Americans was close for a time, but the United States' ascending supremacy in military might enabled Washington officials to start calling more of the shots. Tension rose between U.S. officials and their British counterparts as the Americans came to resent their British colleagues' condescension toward their neophyte partners. In addition, U.S. intelligence offices, especially the FBI, feared Soviet penetration of London's espionage service by turncoat establishment figures. This fear was borne out by the facts after the war, when several Englishmen from elite circles defected and fled to Moscow to escape prosecution. Before those sensational defections, Washington officials had grown more circumspect about close collaboration with the British Security Coordination.[8]

A handful of Washington officials, on the other hand, embraced such British tactics as commando raids, behind-the-lines sabotage, and small-unit resistance cells to sap their enemies' strength and morale. Initially, they looked to the British SOE for example and guidance. With its long tradition of a powerful navy and small peace-time army, Britain historically resorted to irregular warfare from time to time. No British schoolchild escaped the stirring lessons of the Duke of Wellington's campaign in Spain during the Napoleonic Wars. In the course of his Peninsula Campaign, the Iron Duke and the British military establishment utilized irregular warfare and cooperated with Spanish guerrillas against the French invasion in the early nineteenth century. While the British army's involvement with irregular warfare was historically episodic, their leadership grasped its utility in the days following the calamitous retreat from Dunkirk. Churchill and others resorted to covert operations across the English Channel, lacking other options to hit back at the German occupation of Europe.

Officials within the Franklin D. Roosevelt administration also recognized the necessity of gathering, culling, and analyzing a tidal wave of intelligence. Roosevelt needed little convincing about the necessity for forming a clearinghouse to sort through the plethora of intelligence and information pouring in from the battlefronts. Likewise, the administration understood that the United States needed an office dedicated to espionage, subversion, sabotage, propaganda, and other activities usually regarded as un-American by the gentlemanly establishment.

Under the leadership of William J. Donovan, the White House first set up the Coordinator of Information (COI) and then its more significant successor, the OSS—the forerunner of the CIA. During a fact-finding trip to Britain in 1941, Donovan had been impressed with the British ability to integrate several separate intelligence-type functions. Specifically, he saw significant merit in the coordination of intelligence, counterintelligence, and propaganda activities along with subversive operations carried out behind enemy lines in Nazi-occupied Europe. Donovan, a wealthy Wall Street lawyer and World War I Medal of Honor winner, prevailed on Roosevelt to form the COI to coordinate the flow of intelligence from the Army, Navy, FBI, and State Department. The president wanted an end to rivalry among the competing intelligence sections. Each possessed its own particular orientation and code-breaking offices, which it jealously guarded from what was perceived as interference.

President Roosevelt trusted Donovan, who was known as "Wild Bill" by friends and foes alike, although there was disagreement on the origin of the nickname. Some claimed it came from his wild antics on the football field. A recent biographer holds that the former Republican Party official picked up the sobriquet during World War I for his running stamina over arduous terrain at thirty-five years of age.[9] On the bureaucratic field, however, Donovan was only partially effective in coordinating the flow of information from rivalrous government departments. In its short-lived existence, the COI also encompassed counterpropaganda and unconventional warfare functions.

Unwieldy with too many responsibilities and riven with personality conflicts, the COI was dissolved by Roosevelt into two separate entities. The Office of War Information took over "white" propaganda responsibilities to promote America's fight for democracy and freedom from tyranny. This information came from known sources. Except in Latin America, the Office of War Information disseminated information and proselytized democratic values in the ideological conflict with fascism around the globe. The State Department had similar responsibilities for the Western Hemisphere.

The Army took over the so-called black propaganda efforts. Eventually, this function came under the Morale Operations Branch of the OSS. This form of propaganda was disseminated by sham fronts or concealed sources and aimed to lower enemy morale or to induce troops to surrender. In short, it was psychological warfare. The branch fabricated rumors about Hitler's health and sanity; printed morale-lowering posters; and published fake newspapers to generate dissension, divisions, and defeatism within Axis ranks. Psychological warfare operations evolved into a key strategic element during World War II, recognized by many commanders as a critical factor in battling Axis forces.[10]

The White House also established the Office of Strategic Services in mid-1942, with Donovan in charge. The OSS assumed the subversive warfare functions of sabotage and guerrilla warfare operations, run by indigenous personnel, behind the enemy's front lines. These native units were organized, trained, equipped, and guided by American operatives. The OSS also oversaw its own Special Operations Branch, which executed military operations in Europe and Asia. Because the OSS was a civilian organization, it relied on the military for personnel, arms, and airlift capability to carry out such operations. Like its CIA successor, the Office of Strategic Services carried out the intelligence function of collecting and analyzing information while it conducted covert, paramilitary actions.

The imaginative Donovan organized the OSS into three functions: intelligence, special operations, and training. At its peak size, the OSS encompassed some 13,000 employees, with about 7,500 stationed abroad.[11] Just as Nathan Hale had blurred the line between soldier and spy in the 1770s, the OSS's cloak-and-dagger operators eroded the soldier-spy separation and embodied both roles. Years later it bequeathed the dual tasks to its heir, the Central Intelligence Agency. The OSS-trained forces conducted destructive attacks within occupied France, Norway, and the Balkans. The OSS and Britain's SOE formed the celebrated Jedburgh teams, which parachuted into France to join the French Resistance to assist the inland offensive after the U.S. landings on the Normandy coast.[12] In Asia, the OSS instructed the anti-Japanese resistance in Indochina and Burma. The famed Detachment 101 trained some eleven thousand Kachin tribesmen in Burma, where they served as a vanguard to the Allied advance in 1944 by plunging well ahead of the main combat forces to gather intelligence, sabotage key installations, and sow demoralizing rumors. Members of the OSS's Deer Team trained and mentored the Viet Minh to forge an effective resistance to Japan's occupation of Vietnam. After the Japanese surrender, the Viet Minh turned their guns on the returning French colonial forces.

It can be said without exaggeration that other Washington departments opposed the creation of the OSS because it was a potential competitor for resources, missions, and prestige. The military services and the FBI in particular resisted the formation and resourcing of Donovan's infant agency. Army and civilian officials also resented Donovan's close relationship with Roosevelt. The president protected his protégé and interceded on his behalf even with General George C. Marshall, the Army chief of staff. To rein in the OSS, Marshall kept the spy-sabotage organization reporting to his staff rather than allowing it to function as a freestanding organization.[13] The military, however, furnished manpower and equipment to the OSS at Roosevelt's urging. In one major exception, the Joint Chiefs of Staff (JCS) authorized the OSS to operate U.S. commando units in the enemy's rear areas in late 1942. Wearing uniforms, the OSS organized several operational groups, which fought alongside partisans in China, France, Greece, Italy, Malaya, Norway, and Yugoslavia. For the most part, the OSS trained, guided, and armed local forces to attack targets behind the enemy's front lines. Thus the OSS teams prefigured today's Special Forces detachments in organizing, training, and directing host-nation forces as resistance movements.[14]

The Office of Strategic Services' achievements during the 1941–45 war were noteworthy but hardly decisive in winning that titanic struggle. Its successor agency, the CIA, did embrace Donovan's vision of a military offensive in depth—fielding operatives behind enemy lines for support of the military's main operations. At war's end, the OSS was hastily dismantled along with much of the regular armed forces. Some OSS personnel migrated to other government departments, including the Department of State and the then War Department. Conforming to its past tradition, America rapidly demobilized the vast array of armed forces it had marshaled after Pearl Harbor. Yet the OSS idea, and more particularly the role of William Donovan, lived on in the creation of the CIA and the Army's Special Forces. In his informative book *U.S. Army Special Warfare: Its Origins*, Alfred Paddock wrote that "Donovan must be considered the spiritual father of Army unconventional warfare."[15] Neither Donovan's inspiration nor the OSS model lay interred for long in the post–World War II era.

The Rise of the Permanent U.S. Security Apparatus

Almost three-quarters of a century removed from the Soviet Union's deadly threat to the United States and its West European allies, it is hard to comprehend the fear and loathing Americans felt toward the Kremlin after World War II. From 1945 onward, the Soviet Union amassed huge conventional armies and acquired enough nuclear arms to obliterate the United States many times over. Nothing in today's galaxy of threats comes close to the ominous foreboding engendered by an apocalyptical clash between two nuclear-armed titans during the 1950s and 1960s. Washington interpreted the defeat of the Axis powers as an end point. Moscow viewed it as simply another milestone on its march toward global hegemony and pushed the belligerence envelope menacingly in the immediate years after the war. Soviet Russia saw itself hemmed in and challenged by capitalist and imperialist countries. Almost overnight, the United States and the Soviet Union went from being allies to adversaries, although this transformation had been earlier detected by a few keen observers, such as Winston Churchill.[16]

Within only a couple of years after Germany's and Italy's surrender, the Kremlin consolidated its Communist rule in Eastern Europe; crushed Czechoslovakia's independence; triggered a nuclear device; blockaded Berlin from the West; and threatened Greece, Turkey, and Iran with subversion or intervention. In Asia, China fell to Communism in 1949, and with Stalin's approval, Communist North Korea invaded South Korea in 1950. The rapidity of these Soviet-generated threats reinforced Moscow's existential nuclear risk to the West. The enormity of the Soviet challenges alarmed American civilian and military leaders. The sheer size and power of the Red Army garrisoned across Europe brought down an Iron Curtain from the Baltic to the Adriatic. A U.S. ground counterattack against such a formidable land force was nearly unthinkable. In response, Washington opted for a nuclear-armed containment strategy against further Soviet aggression. The Soviet-American standoff devolved into the Cold War, with smaller hot conflicts on the peripheries of their respective spheres.

In light of these geopolitical developments, Washington realized that the United States needed both a centralized intelligence service and specialized military forces, although these realizations came not in equal measure. Washington first set about erecting an intelligence apparatus, which also picked up the rump, covert paramilitary capabilities from the disbanded OSS. The world was far too dangerous to return to the interwar period of disarmament and isolation.

Just three months after disbanding the Office of Strategic Services in January 1946, President Harry Truman signed into existence the Central Intelligence Group, a short-lived, transitional office that paved the way for the Central Intelligence Agency. The War Department transferred its Strategic Service Unit to the intelligence group and with it the remaining OSS resources. In 1947, Congress passed the National Security Act, which ushered in the Central Intelligence Agency as an independent agency. Like the OSS, this new agency initially took up the task of collecting and analyzing intelligence so as to minimize friction between competing military and civilian intelligence branches.[17]

The National Security Act also set up the National Security Council (NSC) and gave the CIA the task of providing intelligence and analysis to it. The National Security Council functioned as a forum inside the White House to advise the president on foreign policy and national security issues. Furthermore, the act designated the CIA to carry out "services of common concern" and to "perform such other functions and duties as the NSC from time to time directs." These vague requirements, coupled with explicit directives, over time expanded the CIA's covert activities. Also in 1947, the National Security Council issued a directive known as NSC4, which gave the CIA responsibility for covert psychological operations. In a secret annex, NSC4A, the National Security Council opened the way for the CIA to be in the covert business.[18] By late 1948, the CIA acquired a limited clandestine function in the innocuous-sounding Office of Policy

Coordination under Frank Wisner, who had been an OSS station chief in Romania during the war.[19]

The Korean War (1950–53) necessitated expanding the Office of Policy Coordination's paramilitary capabilities along with accruing manpower, overseas stations, and bigger budgets. Together with other enhanced responsibilities and growth, the CIA grew sixfold in its first six years of existence. Its clandestine service developed into the largest section in the agency.[20] As the covert operations' component enlarged, it bore the imprint of the Office of Strategic Services. Former OSS personnel flocked to the welcome embrace of the CIA as the war of words heated up with Moscow.

Both Cold War protagonists resorted to heavy doses of propaganda, for the nature of the global struggle was part ideological war between Marxist-Leninist doctrines and liberal democratic values. The pitched battle of ideas demanded that the United States respond to the Kremlin's disinformation campaign and ideological messages. As the Pentagon made the military threat posed by Communism's territorial expansion an urgent priority, it relied on the CIA to build its own apparatus to combat propaganda and to conduct unconventional military operations inside the Soviet bloc. Under the direction of the National Security Council, the Central Intelligence Agency and its Office of Policy Coordination had taken the lead in developing psychological and unconventional warfare.

The U.S. military, by contrast, focused on conventional warfare. For the top brass, especially in the Army, hostility toward "unsoldierly" guerrilla warfare and covert operations did not fade with the end of World War II. The Joint Chiefs of Staff, in fact, passed the responsibility for training and supporting resistance movements against Communist encroachments to the CIA in peace time. The Army assisted these efforts only in limited ways. By 1950 the CIA was assuming responsibility for all psychological warfare and covert operations behind the enemy's front lines. The Army's attitude, however, shifted dramatically toward the spurned activities, and it came to embrace them, at least for a while. What caused the radical shift? In a word, war. War, in this case the Korean War, made a difference to the Pentagon about operations affecting the conflict's outcome.

The surprise, across-the-border invasion by Communist North Korea into an inadequately defended South Korea in 1950 rekindled the top brass's interest in psychological warfare techniques to accompany military operations. The Pentagon realized from the World War II experience that psychological operations could demoralize or convince enemy soldiers to surrender or desert their ranks. Thus, it delivered propaganda to the enemy's front lines via airborne leaflets. The Pentagon also turned to radio broadcasts in the Korean language to arouse anti-Chinese feelings after China entered the war.

With the onset of the Korean conflict, the Pentagon wanted to carry out its own psychological operations rather than trust them to civilian departments. Therefore, the Department of Defense established the Office of the Chief of Psychological Warfare (OCPW) in late 1950. Interestingly, the OCPW's mission included "special operations" as well as psychological warfare. The military regulations that set up the OCPW outlined its mission: to "formulate and develop psychological and *special operations* (emphasis added) plans for the Army in consonance with established policy and to recommend policies for and supervise the execution of the Department of Army programs in those fields."[21]

Herein lay the genesis of the Special Operations Forces. The OCPW's initial purpose clearly centered on psychological warfare capabilities. But the mission statement incorporated "special operations" as well. It was the legendary Army brigadier general Robert McClure who put flesh on the OCPW's skeleton. General McClure had gained experience and expertise in psychological warfare while serving under General Dwight Eisenhower in North Africa and Europe. Years later he applied the past war's techniques to the OCPW in a new conflict. He structured the OCPW into three main sections—Requirements, Special Operations, and Psychological Operations. The Requirements Division handled personnel, training, and logistical duties in support of the two other divisions. Special Operations dealt with unconventional warfare, as was understood by the OSS to mean readying and arming partisans, or local forces, to fight in the enemy's rear. McClure and his staff set down plans and implemented policies for the Office of the Chief of Psychological Operations. In a short span, their frantic efforts yielded the establishment of the Psychological Warfare Center, the formation of the Tenth Special Forces Group, and the co-location of these two entities within one center at Fort Bragg, North Carolina.

Just as the fighting in Korea boosted the military's expertise in propaganda enterprises and led to Special Operations groups, it also witnessed the continuation of the Central Intelligence Agency's OSS-type endeavors on the embattled peninsula. Among the CIA's covert activities was intelligence collection, assistance to downed U.S. pilots for escape, and sabotage operations, plus limited partisan operations behind North Korean lines. These unconventional warfare activities, as might be expected, overlapped with the U.S. Army's comparable operations and resulted in eventual tension between the two.

To incite and sustain effective behind-the-lines actions, America's Eighth Army assigned officers and enlisted men (who often had little background in unconventional tactics) to train and direct the civilian population in guerrilla-type tactics. These unconventional forces were initially supervised by an ad hoc section within the Eighth Army's operations staff, or G-3, and were known initially as the Miscellaneous Group. The group set out to train, coordinate, and supply Koreans in partisan warfare waged by individuals and groups that engaged in sabotage in areas behind the battlefield. By war's end, the forces totaled more than five thousand strong. They operated both within North Korea and along its coast, striking enemy units with ambushes, raids, and brief in-and-out amphibious assaults. U.S. military personnel sometimes accompanied the three main partisan formations, which were designated Leopard, Wolf Pack, and Kirkland.[22]

Friction quickly arose between the Army's Office of Chief of Psychological Warfare and the Central Intelligence Agency. As an Army champion, OCPW's McClure disapproved of the CIA's autonomous role in the Korean conflict. In his judgment, the CIA officers took orders or asked permission from their Langley, Virginia, headquarters before cooperating with Eighth Army staff. McClure also believed that the CIA prioritized intelligence collection and analysis over running unconventional warfare operations behind the enemy's front lines. Although the CIA did use military personnel in its teams and engaged in limited secret missions in rear areas similar to the Eighth Army, it did so without adequate liaison with the regular U.S. ground forces. The general wanted the spy agency to be closely integrated into a joint task force with the military for better coordination. General McClure and his OCPW staff also believed that unconventional warfare was underappreciated and underutilized by the regular Army. They thought "special operations" (by which they meant guerrilla tactics performed by Americans or indigenous personnel) went undercoordinated with the larger conventional war.

Thus, unconventional practices lacked real consequence for the Korean War effort.

McClure and his OCPW won a partial victory by the time of the 1953 armistice. The Army hierarchy generally accepted the utility of psychological warfare for the success of ground combat. The Army command also accepted its separation from subordination to the G-3 staff, which was a goal of McClure's. Instead, the Army agreed to the creation of a separate Psychological Warfare Center at Ft. Bragg.

The OCPW's specialized-soldiers component also evolved during the Korean War. McClure enlisted Army officers with OSS experience in wartime France and Asia for his Special Operations Division. He also tapped a handful of seasoned Army officers who ran guerrilla operations within North Korea. These officers held that because the Army bore responsibility for winning land wars, it must not delegate behind-enemy-lines actions to a civilian agency, that is, the CIA. Almost by default, it stepped into the breach left in the nation's security architecture without a department to organize clandestine paramilitary activities after the disbanding of the Office of Strategic Services. The Army and the Pentagon itself recognized the CIA's legitimacy and skill in organizing, funding, and directing limited paramilitary activities during peace time. But once hostilities were declared, the Pentagon reasoned, it must take control of unconventional military enterprises. Because the Pentagon changed its attitude about training and fielding specialized forces, it moved to gain control from the CIA of these formerly spurned operations. Naturally, hard feelings arose in both military and intelligence communities about this division of labor.

Inside the OCPW's Special Operations Division, a tiny officer corps resolved to chart a course for the Army to assume operations to the rear of the battlefield. They developed doctrine, concepts, and studies for special forces members to stand up and train indigenous resistance movements inside enemy-controlled terrain. These specialized troops were less interested in the heroic battleground engagements celebrated by direct-action forces such as the Rangers or other commando-type units, which directly confronted hostile forces in firefights. Rather, the specialized forces worked to train and guide local forces so they, not their American mentors, would ultimately pull the triggers on the enemy. The war in Korea weighed heavily in their thinking, but the Red Army's occupation of Eastern Europe was also never far from their thoughts. The Army's interest in covert warfare benefited from the support of Secretary of War Robert Patterson, who saw the need for OSS-type units and activities. By mid-1950, Secretary of the Army Frank Pace Jr. also recognized the need for psychological and unconventional warfare. His backing of the OCPW proved crucial not just for the Korean conflict but also for secret plans regarding Soviet-dominated Eastern Europe.[23] Therefore, the Army's push for Special Forces came not from the CIA but rather from the international exigencies of the Cold War.

As such, OCPW's Special Operations Division turned its attention to deep penetration and long-range reconnaissance as well as subversion and sabotage inside Soviet-occupied countries. The Special Operations staff grasped the untapped potential in newly arrived American immigrants, many of whom were first- or second-generation citizens; they spoke Ukrainian, Polish, German, Serbian, or other East European languages. As recruits, these foreign-language-proficient soldiers could be assigned to and trained for specialized units posted to U.S. Army bases in Europe. In the event of a Soviet attack, these specialized troops would conduct activities to disrupt the Red Army by mounting sabotage or assisting local anti-Russian partisans.

Inevitably, mutual suspicion and tension arose between the OCPW and the CIA as the Army's Psychological Warfare Center staff struggled to form its own specialized units to engage in missions similar to those currently carried out by the civilian spy agency. One point to remember here is that the degree of debate centered on whether a state of war or peace prevailed. During wartime, the Pentagon believed it was accountable for the nation's victory or defeat. Thus, it demanded control of covert operations in the enemy's rear zones. In peace, the military, as well as the U.S. government, acknowledged the benefit of having a secret civilian agency stage subversive activity inside foreign countries. The two camps' opposing viewpoints eventually led to the issuance of Title 10 and Title 50 authorities within the U.S. Code, which delineated each entity's roles and missions—a topic to be subsequently discussed.

A second major point requires only brief note because it is so obvious and so recurring. The stakes between the CIA and the Pentagon repeatedly involved fights over political turf, budgeted funds, and even prestige. These competitions, I must emphasize, took place almost entirely at the upper levels of the bureaucracy, not by troops in the Special Operations Forces or officers in the Central Intelligence Agency on the ground. In war zones, the special warfare operators and CIA field officers depended on each other for survival, or at least for mutual support, to accomplish a mission. Cooperation stood as a necessity, not bureaucratic rivalry. In the lofty corridors of power, the game could be less harmonious.

As Brigadier General McClure prepared to build a separate training center for psychological and unconventional warfare, Frank Wisner, equally strong willed, raised issues from his Office of Policy Coordination within the CIA. By mid-1951, after several discussions, the two camps reached a tentative agreement on unconventional warfare. McClure, Wisner, and their respective staffs agreed to implement an official liaison between the two offices to coordinate research activities. This settlement represented one among numerous attempts to work out understandings between the two communities.[24]

General McClure's bureaucratic skirmishes were not limited to the CIA and its Office of Policy Coordination. Even within the Army, many mainstream officers remained skeptical about the cost-benefit value of devoting resources to guerrilla raids and sabotage actions away from the front lines. Some military brass regarded such operations as, at best, "sideshows" and, at worst, diversions from the main objective of closing with and destroying the enemy force.[25] Any sustained discussion of these wrangles takes the reader well beyond the scope of this monograph, but not mentioning them at all would give rise to a false picture of harmonious acceptance by the conventional armed forces. Suffice to say here that the hurdles facing Special Forces proved as high as they did for other units within the overall Special Operations Forces as we know them today. These interservice and interagency rivalries persisted and will be touched on briefly in later paragraphs.

Once the Psychological Warfare Center was launched and designated as a service school in 1952, it moved to activate the same broad organizational structure of its progenitor, the Office of the Chief of Psychological Warfare, as noted above. The center set up a Psychological Operations Department and a Special Forces Department. It was the latter department that spawned the Tenth Special Forces Group. In setting up this unit, McClure and his officers stressed the distinction between the Rangers of World War II and Korean War vintage and what they meant by "special forces." Rangers performed penetration and infiltration of enemy lines for short durations to raid and harass targets.

They relied on U.S. personnel and utilized no foreign soldiers in their ranks. Per contra, the early formulators of the Special Forces made plain their objective to incorporate local men into their groups to carry out long-duration missions behind enemy lines. Their inspiration derived from the OSS operational groups during World War II. Special Forces operators latched onto the mission of organizing, training, arming, and directing these indigenous units in attacks against the enemy's flanks and rear. The distinctions were sometimes lost on conventional officers who confused the roles and missions of soldiers outside the regular Army framework.

All in all, the 1950s turned out to be a dispiriting decade for Special Forces in the Army. The Tenth Special Forces Group did deploy to Germany in late 1953. It left a stay-behind cadre, which formed the Seventy-Seventh Special Forces Group at Fort Bragg. A few detachments established the First Special Group in Okinawa. But the manpower reductions Army-wide during the decade also brought special warriors in the Army to the brink of extinction. They stood at a mere two thousand personnel by 1960, a small enough number to eliminate without much public outcry.

The early 1960s began a better decade for the Special Forces as President John Kennedy became a white knight of sorts. Kennedy considered direct conflict with the Soviet Union as unlikely and catastrophic because of the U.S. strategy of relying exclusively on the atom bomb to deter Moscow from aggression. Direct conventional war could well escalate to either a nuclear abyss or a humiliating stand-down by Washington to avoid such a nightmare war. Kennedy foresaw "another type of war, new in its intensity, ancient in its origins—war by guerrillas, subversives, and insurgents, assassins; war by ambush instead of by combat; by infiltration instead of aggression." He added that it would require "a whole new kind of strategy, a wholly different kind of force, and therefore a new and wholly different kind of military training."[26] Kennedy was responding to Soviet leader Nikita Khrushchev's support of insurgent wars of national liberation in the non-Western world.

President Kennedy was prophetic in his vision of future conflict. He promoted the Special Forces mission. He even ensured that the Special Forces could wear their distinctive green berets, which became synonymous with these units for a while. Today's Special Forces only occasionally refer to themselves as Green Berets, so the term is mostly reminiscent of the Vietnam era. It was also during Kennedy's presidency that the United States formed the first U.S. Navy SEALs as part of the emerging specialized warriors of the post–World War II period. Although the SEALs' lineage is most directly traceable to the Underwater Demolition Teams of World War II fame, the contemporary-day SEALs possess the capability to operate from the sea, air, or land. The Underwater Demolition Teams performed reconnaissance and direct-action operations, which form the basis of the SEALs' current repertoire. But SEALs also undertake training, counterterror, and hostage-rescue missions. Like the Army Special Forces, the SEALs saw a lot of action during the Vietnam War, where they sometimes cooperated with CIA field officers. Some SEALs moved over to the Phoenix Program and worked with the CIA to extirpate the National Liberation Front/Viet Cong infrastructure operating in the countryside.[27] We now turn to a more in-depth discussion of the Special Forces–CIA collaboration during the Vietnam War.

chapter three

Specialized Soldiering and Intelligence Operatives in the Vietnam War

A CHANGE IN MARTIAL FORTUNES during the 1960s rescued Special Forces units from obscurity and even possible disbandment. The Cold War entered a new phase with Moscow's (and sometimes Beijing's) backing of Marxist "national liberation" movements in the non-Western world. These movements fought insurgencies against European colonial governments, some of which were allied to Washington. Other Marxist revolutionary leaders waged low-intensity conflicts against pro-American regimes in Latin America as well as Africa and Asia. The enormous nuclear arsenals relied on to check a Soviet offensive into the European heartland were unsuited to defeat the slow-burning brushfire wars. The Marxist revolutionaries took to the remote forests or mountains to elude and to wear down their conventional opponents. Besieged governments looked to the United States to defeat the Communist-backed tide overrunning their lands with insurgency. In these conflicts, the doctrine of mutual assured destruction with nuclear weapons proved ineffective and unrealistic. Bombing jungles or highland plateaus to kill insurgents was useless. Thus, the Green Berets and other special operations units took up the counterinsurgency mission, as envisioned by President Kennedy.

America's widest application of counterinsurgency warfare after the Philippine insurrection took place in South Vietnam. American intervention began with aid in 1950 to the beleaguered French forces fighting against the North Vietnamese insurgents known as the Viet Minh. By that time the Viet Minh were a seasoned guerrilla force, having fought Japan during World War II and then France, which tried to reassert colonial control over Indochina following the war. Outnumbered by the insurgents, France decided to leave Vietnam following its defeat at the epic battle of Dien Bien Phu in 1954. After the division of Vietnam into South Vietnam and the Communist-dominated North Vietnam in the 1954 Geneva Accords, the United States realigned its support from the departing French to the defense of the South Vietnamese government. Washington hoped to block the Communist subversion of all Indochina. Hardly had the ink dried on the accords than North Vietnam infiltrated Communist cadres and guerrillas into its southern neighbor to aid the Viet Cong (VC) insurgents to topple the Saigon government by subverting the countryside. To rally the population against the Saigon government and its U.S. backers, the Viet Cong fabricated a National Liberation Front of the South Vietnamese Communist Party to rally the population to their anti-American cause.

Through terror and intimidation, the VC destroyed Saigon's governance structure and stitched together a parallel civic apparatus among the rural populations. The village-level shadow governments levied taxes, imposed harsh Communist rule, dispensed limited social services, and set up an intelligence network to keep tabs on Saigon's military and to spy on the population so as to kill government officials and informants. The Communist cadres also raised two types of military units—"local" auxiliaries and "main" force companies and battalions—to engage Saigon and later American combat troops. As past masters of insurgent warfare, the VC engaged in classic guerrilla tactics of hit-and-run raids, ambushes, and booby traps calculated to frustrate, bleed, demoralize, and emasculate progovernment conventional forces rather than attempt to defeat them in a straight-up battle. This low-intensity conflict of pinprick attacks and political indoctrination called for a counteroffensive far different from the regular World War II warfare. In short, Communist subversive warfare waged by national liberation movements, such as the Viet Cong, demanded an unconventional response, one that could be answered by the Green Berets and other special military forces.

Much of current U.S. counterinsurgency doctrine and practice are rooted in the Vietnam War experience. But many lessons of that Southeast Asian conflict were almost deliberately ignored then so as to concentrate on a possible large-scale conventional war in Europe, which never materialized. Later, however, the Vietnam insurgency exerted an influence on the fighting in Iraq and Afghanistan as its history was analyzed three decades afterward. The drafters of the 2006 *U.S. Army/Marine Corps Counterinsurgency Field Manual 3–24* drew frequently on lessons from America's most frustrating war of the twentieth century.[1]

One dimension of the Vietnam War that requires review is the SOF-CIA interaction. Beginning before the U.S. military engagement reached large-scale proportions after mid-1965, a close, even symbiotic, relationship developed between the Central Intelligence Agency and Special Forces. As French forces retreated from Indochina in the wake of the Geneva Accords, Washington stepped into the growing political vacuum. To rally support among ethnic minorities for the Saigon government and to impede the infiltration of North Vietnamese cadre and arms flowing southward, the U.S. Army dispatched Special Forces to the remote central highlands to aid CIA efforts. This effort came about with the 1962 issuance of National Security Action Memorandum NSAM 162, which assigned Special Forces troops "to support CIA covert paramilitary operations" in Vietnam.[2]

As a prelude to this mission, Special Forces had been deployed to neighboring Laos as part of Operation White Star for the purpose of assisting the population to resist the Communist Pathet Lao in the late 1950s. The operation, run by legendary Army colonel Arthur "Bull" Simons, trained the indigenous Kha tribesmen to fight the Pathet Lao with guerrilla tactics.[3] In addition, the United States started backing Thailand's anti-Communist counterinsurgency in the late 1950s. Special Forces teams operating under CIA direction trained Thai police and border patrols to resist subversion.[4]

The Agency also ran an effective paramilitary program in neighboring Laos during the Lyndon Johnson administration. Starting in July 1959, Special Forces teams joined French advisers, who were still training the Laotian army. The American troops wore civilian clothes and carried civilian identification cards. The CIA paid them to maintain a "nonmilitary" presence.[5] There, they aided Vang Pao, the famed Hmong military leader, in resisting a Communist takeover of the kingdom until the complete American combat withdrawal from Indochina by April 1973. The Green Beret–CIA mission pulled back from Laos in 1962 in accordance with the Geneva Convention. From there, Green Berets trained South Vietnamese Special Forces as well as ethnic groups to safeguard villages and harass and attack Viet Cong guerrillas.

In late 1961, a small Special Forces detachment walked into a Rhade village to assist the population in their resistance to the Viet Cong. The Rhade were the dominant tribe within the Montagnard ethnic minority. The Special Forces worked under the CIA in the

Civilian Irregular Defense Groups (CIDGs). Their purpose was to recruit, organize, train, arm, and direct Montagnard villagers to offer stiffer resistance to the Viet Cong, who passed through villagers' lands and coerced them into joining the insurgency. In short, the Americans helped the Montagnards protect themselves. The Green Berets did this by winning their trust through sharing village life and everyday hardships. They also sought to improve the daily lot of the Montagnards by setting up modest dispensaries, teaching the use of simple tools, and transferring effective farming techniques to the seminomadic villagers. They also trained Montagnards as village health and medical workers.[6] These limited but classic hearts-and-minds methods won over the highlanders. A year later, CIDG mustered approximately thirty-eight thousand militiamen trained in defense of their villages.[7] Its methods thereby enshrined the "by, with, or through" practice that became the hallmark of counterinsurgency in the course of the Iraq and Afghanistan wars decades later.

For its part, the Central Intelligence Agency had been involved in paramilitary operations prior to the arrival of the first Special Forces personnel to the Vietnam highlands. CIA political action teams also worked among the Vietnamese coastal communities to facilitate the spread of the central government's services to them as a way to strengthen the bond between rural peoples and their government in Saigon.[8] Then the CIA initiated similar programs in the Central Highlands before turning them over to Special Forces soldiers. The CIA's adaptable supply system and its ready money in small bills imparted flexibility and latitude to the Special Forces to develop their civil-defense counterinsurgency practices. The CIA-initiated and SOF-run pacification mission worked wonders. Personnel from both security entities understood the core principle of building trust with the host country's populations.[9] The efforts yielded a kind of self-defense focus among indigenous people that counterinsurgent practitioners strive to attain. As Douglas Blaufarb wrote in his valuable book, *The Counterinsurgency Era: U.S. Doctrine and Performance:*

> In a little more than thirteen months some thirty-eight thousand tribesmen were armed and over two hundred villages were incorporated into the scheme [Village Defense Program] with a population of about three hundred thousand. The inducement for the tribespeople was self-protection against the Viet Cong together with such programs as training for medical aides, dispensaries, education, and similar small-scale improvement in their lives.[10]

In reviewing the progress of the Civilian Irregular Defense Groups, the special assistant to the chief of staff for Special Warfare Activities reported in 1963: "The CIDG program holds the key to the attainment of the ultimate goal of a free, stable, and secure Vietnam."[11]

Events well beyond Indochina adversely impacted the CIA's role among the South Vietnamese self-defense groups, however. In 1961 the CIA-run Bay of Pigs debacle, in which the Defense Department played only a small part, resulted in a humiliation for the young John F. Kennedy administration. As a result, President Kennedy asked retired general Maxwell D. Taylor to draw lessons from the abortive Cuban-exile invasion. Among the Taylor Commission's observations was one that singled out the CIA's role in paramilitary activities. The commission noted that the CIA lacked sufficient staff, logistical capability, and coordinating capacity across air, land, and sea environments. It also lacked a clearly defined chain of command to orchestrate the exiles' beach landing. Henceforth, the commission advised, the

CIA should turn over covert paramilitary missions to the Pentagon once they reached large-scale enterprises.[12]

Clearly, the tasks of training, arming, and guiding tens of thousands of ethnic minorities and South Vietnamese forces by 1963 required a transfer from the CIA to the Defense Department. By midpoint of that year, the operational size of the CIA-trained Montagnard militias surpassed the threshold established by the Taylor Commission after the Bay of Pigs. For its part, the Army also wanted to move the Special Forces out from under the CIA and to switch the Green Beret–trained locals from counterinsurgency pacification to aggressive offensive patrols and ambushes.[13]

Before the turnover, the Special Forces–CIA collaboration functioned well. The Army assigned Special Forces detachments to work with CIA case officers. About 450 Green Berets trained locals and lived in austere hamlets and villages. The various training programs, presided over by the CIA, were transferred to the Army in Operation Switchback in 1963. Head CIA officer in Vietnam William Colby later wrote: "It was plain that the informal and direct channels that the CIA used to move logistics, weapons, and money to the point of use were not available to the military."[14] The Green Berets had warmed to the Agency's flexibility in transferring carbines, supplies, and money for civic and humanitarian projects. Whereas the Army's system was bound up in bureaucracy, the CIA logistical chain was responsive and adaptable to the Green Berets' requirements.[15]

When the Military Assistance Command Vietnam (MACV), the overarching military command, assumed authority over the Special Forces, the transition was far from easy. A former OSS hand, William Colby, who had been the CIA station chief (1959–62), wrote that "it became clear that the transfer could not be simple."[16] That was an understatement of the trials ahead. Operation Switchback entailed not just a change in paymaster and logistician but also a dramatic reorientation in mission.

The joint Special Forces–CIA teamwork forged an effective counterinsurgency program. The two entities stressed strong rural communities working from the bottom up. They trained, aided, and armed local inhabitants to fashion part-time home guards to defend themselves and to extend their defensive perimeters much like French marshal Hubert Lyautey's celebrated *tache d'huile* ("oil spot") strategy. This counterinsurgency technique envisioned the expanding of one oil splotch to another. The spreading and connecting oil spots, in time, would cover the cloth, leaving no room for the insurgents to operate. Such pacification operations also denied food, intelligence, and recruits to the Viet Cong. The aim centered on engaging villagers in their own defense rather than going after and killing VC guerrillas. As for the CIA, it did not totally abandon the counterinsurgency efforts. Rather, its paramilitary officers worked with South Vietnamese officials and police to eradicate the Viet Cong cadre in the countryside.[17]

After the Operation Switchback transfer, the MACV decided that the community's defensive pacification was far too passive. Accordingly, it moved to train and deploy Montagnards as full-time "strike forces" for offensive operations against infiltrating North Vietnamese. This transformation required stationing the strike forces in isolated bases along the Laotian and Cambodian borders to interdict the infiltrators by using relentless patrols and highly kinetic actions. The villagers, in short, changed from a village defense militia to a commando force. Colby assessed the transformation thusly: "We decided to fight our kind of war rather than the kind the enemy was fighting."[18] A Communist people's war demanded a counterinsurgency strategy of pacification, security for villagers, and trust building in order to connect rural areas with the central government. But MACV opted for an offensive strategy.

In time, the Montagnards became less effective in their new role and postings distant from their home villages. Village protection fell by the wayside as the Montagnards and the CIDGs were conventionalized into strike units. Saigon also played a role in derailing the promising local defensive militias. The South Vietnamese government deeply disliked the mountain people, and it distrusted the Special Forces organizers. The animosities lit a powder keg. Resentful of their South Vietnamese overlords, who regarded the ethnic minority as inferior and dangerous, the Montagnards staged a rebellion. In the end, conventionalizing the villagers undermined the once-promising SOF-CIA partnership among the Montagnards.[19] Colby, who went from CIA station chief in Saigon to years later the director of Central Intelligence, bitterly reflected on the Agency's view of the conventional military's handling counterinsurgency: "After the Bay of Pigs we turned the war over to the military and they screwed it up."[20]

Another factor in turning over paramilitary-type operations to the Army stemmed from CIA failures to infiltrate Vietnamese agents into North Vietnam to disrupt its war making and its infiltration of the South. Unlike 1940s' France, Indochina, or the more permissive Axis-occupied countries of World War II, the People's Republic of Vietnam was truly a denied area, locked down securely against foreign intervention. Infiltration and survival were considered nearly impossible. While the CIA was only too happy to get out from under the failing North Vietnam infiltration program, it was less interested in handing over its "first string" intelligence officers to the MACV's euphemistically relabeled Studies and Observation Group (SOG), formerly named the Special Operations Group. The newly re-formed SOG enlisted Green Berets, U.S. Navy SEALs, South Vietnamese troops, and some CIA assistance in mounting reconnaissance operations into Cambodia and Laos. MACV-SOG ended up running the biggest and most complex unconventional missions the United States had executed since the OSS days.[21]

Thus, the CIA's role in the North Vietnam mission was diminished as the U.S. military presence mounted in the embattled country. Nor did the Agency have an interest in "taking orders from the military," in the words of Richard Shultz in his magisterial book, *The Secret War against Hanoi*.[22] Instead, the Agency was minimally cooperative as it turned its attention to the actions against the Viet Cong within South Vietnam. The Agency was more forthcoming when it came to psychological warfare because it "reflected its indifference"; it did not consider psychological warfare specialists "first string officers."[23] Mostly on its own, MACV-SOG assumed the former CIA infiltration operations into North Vietnam with merely residual Agency backing. SOG's new ownership of the "black" operations in the North opened it to mainstream Army opposition as the senior leadership shared a low opinion of unconventional warfare tactics.[24]

Like their Special Forces counterparts, the U.S. Navy SEALs, as noted earlier, saw extensive combat during the Vietnam War. The SEALs were thrown into the thick of the conflict before the conventional U.S. buildup that started in mid-1965. The SEALs were first deployed to Da Nang and then elsewhere. Like the Green Berets, the SEALs worked with the CIA to infiltrate Vietnamese agents into the North to spark resistance movements.[25] Before and after the CIA turnover of its agent-running operations to MACV, the SEALs were utilized in direct-action missions in the country's swampy riverine terrain. By the mid-1960s, deadly assaults in marshy lands became their daily fare. Their muscular tactics achieved largely unsung fame in rescuing 152 of the 300 freed South Vietnamese prisoners of the Viet Cong over several operations.[26] And finally, like the Special Forces troops, the SEALs benefited from their CIA partnership during the Vietnam War, for it conferred a degree of freedom on the Navy's special warriors that alienated the conventional powers that be.[27]

Back in Washington, a war within a war brewed at the highest military levels. The Joint Chiefs of Staff reflected mainstream military thinking on covert operations against North Vietnam or against its Ho Chi Minh Trail, a manpower and material supply pipeline, which originated in North Vietnam and partially snaked through Laos and Cambodia before entering South Vietnam. The JCS perceived little utility in small-scale attacks on the trail. These "black" operations along the Ho Chi Minh Trail increasingly fell exclusively to the Studies and Observation Group. This secret multiservice force also carried out cross-border attacks after its establishment in mid-1964. The Pentagon chiefs, nevertheless, figured unconventional warfare hardly counted. However much mayhem it sowed or information it gleaned, SOG won little respect among regular military higher-ups. SOG handed over intelligence about North Vietnam's use of the corridor to the South, it destroyed bridges to add delay to the North's resupply efforts, and it ambushed and killed insurgent replacements trekking into the Republic of Vietnam. Conventionally minded generals viewed these actions as pinpricks, not worth the expenditure of vital resources. Yet these same general officers strove to keep the CIA at arm's length from covert military operations while they dragged their feet on implementing SOG plans for conducting raids and ambushes beyond South Vietnamese boundaries.[28] In their resistance, they also bucked the White House and its key occupant, President Kennedy, who, as noted earlier, recognized the applicability of specially trained forces for combating a raging insurgency. As a means to control special warfare actions and yet to appear favorable to them, JCS chairman Earle Wheeler established the Office of the Special Assistant for Counterinsurgency and Special Activities (SACSA) in early 1962. It was first headed by Marine major general Victor "Brute" Krulak, who embraced the mainstream military philosophy on the war in Indochina. Between 1964 and 1972, SACSA oversaw all of SOG's activities. In this way, the top brass reined in the CIA and its own lower-ranking officers who favored more shadow-war tactics. The CIA worked with SOG almost primarily on attacks against the Ho Chi Minh Trail inside Laos.[29]

Within the interagency fights, SACSA sometimes went up against the CIA and the State Department. It was handicapped in bureaucratic feuding by the Pentagon's brass, who put the office under a two-star general, who lacked the same clout as four-star officers. Moreover, the Pentagon chiefs were lukewarm on the SACSA unconventional warfare proposals. Another of SOG's unwelcome ideas—organize resistance movements inside North Vietnam—went nowhere. The State Department and CIA joined the Pentagon in sinking this unconventional plan.[30]

The top U.S. generals in South Vietnam and the Pentagon dragged their feet even in the face of prodding by the Kennedy White House, which championed and authorized unconventional operations against North Vietnam. They beheld little, if any, benefit in sabotage and raids in the North and even less value in fabricating a phantom resistance movement to seed apprehension or internal tension among North Vietnamese security forces. General William Westmoreland, MACV commanding general, also dismissed irregular warfare tactics. Discussing reports of SOG blowing up a bridge, the West Point–trained officer disregarded the military impact as "the enemy just went downstream, say maybe one or two miles, and they'd use another bridge."[31] As for inserting agent teams onto North Vietnamese soil, Westmoreland argued, not unpersuasively, that President Lyndon Johnson opposed a broadening of the war, for it could provoke a Chinese intervention à la Beijing's 1950 invasion into Korea to retrieve the fortunes of the retreating North Korean army.[64] Thus, SOG stayed very subordinate to the overall MACV strategy.

In part, the brass was risk averse to cross-border special operations. The Bay of Pigs debacle cast its shadow over even the military, which escaped blame for the CIA fiasco on the infamous Cuban beach. Their concerns, it must be emphasized, were not meritless. The media and student protestors seized on any perceived expansion of the war. The 1970 Cambodian incursion, for example, sparked massive demonstrations across the United States in which the Kent State shooting of campus protestors rose to iconic status within the antiwar movement. The multistarred commanders were also too set in their ways. By 1965, MACV-SOG redirected its attention from the largely fruitless North Vietnam insertion campaign to next-door Laos. Here the 1962 Geneva Accords handicapped America's counterresponse to Communist penetration from North Vietnam, which was aided by the Soviet Union. In a fanciful attempt to preserve the Laotian status quo among competing parties, the United States agreed to the neutralization of the country. The Communist forces, on the other hand, stepped up infiltration and subversion of the landlocked country, while Moscow, Beijing, and Hanoi proclaimed its neutrality. Their tactics—insinuation of cadres into Laos while proclaiming adherence to the accords—succeeded in a Communist takeover. Laos remains one of the few Communist states in the world today.

Starting in 1965, MACV-SOG worked through the Geneva Accords restrictions. It ran reconnaissance missions that generated intelligence for U.S. bombing runs on the Ho Chi Minh

Trail. The SOG teams of U.S. and South Vietnamese troops captured North Vietnamese personnel for further information to aid air strikes on the north-south conduit. During the late 1960s, SOG crimped North Vietnam's resupply pipeline, and these clandestine operations worried Hanoi. Then, the North Vietnamese launched the Tet Offensive on January 30, 1968, which was a major surprise attack on some one hundred urban centers at the start of the Vietnamese lunar holiday. Militarily, the Tet Offensive failed, costing an estimated forty-five thousand deaths among the North's forces and cadres. Except for the monthlong battle to retake the central city of Hué, the bulk of the provincial capitals and small towns fell within a few days to the U.S.–South Vietnamese counterattack. But symbolically and psychologically, Hanoi scored a political victory, particularly on American campuses and in the news media. The television networks' interpretation of the Tet Offensive deepened doubts within the United States about the wisdom of the war and fueled the antiwar protests in the nation's streets.

Afterward, the Richard Nixon administration turned to what was called the Vietnamization of the war. It trained and equipped the Army of the Republic of Vietnam to stand on its own feet against the insurgency and its North Vietnamese backers. Gradually, the United States withdrew its forces as it negotiated with Hanoi. Once the Paris agreement was signed in January 1973, Washington withdrew the remaining 24,000 troops from the Southeast Asian country. For the next two years, the Republic of South Vietnam more than held its own against a rural insurgency. Then, in April 1975, Hanoi unleashed a large-scale conventional invasion that rapidly overran the South's defenders. America stood on the sidelines. It provided neither air support nor ammunition resupply or spare parts for South Vietnam's defense. Despite the beseeching by President Gerald Ford for assistance to the U.S. ally, the American Congress washed its hands of its erstwhile partner in the anti-Communist struggle. The Army of the Republic of Vietnam collapsed in a matter of weeks.[32] To this day, the media, pundits, and academicians accuse the U.S. military of losing the Southeast Asian war without noting the role played by the U.S. Congress in the strategic loss of an ally.[33]

The SOF–CIA Cooperation in Retrospect

The SOF-CIA liaison during the Vietnam War functioned reasonably well. The normal civilian-military divide was less a factor than the OSS-military divisions of World War II. The fact that some CIA officers came from the SOF ranks mitigated the civilian suit–military uniform division. In remote areas, the two groups depended on each other for survival and for the war's success. They usually shared a similar understanding about how to wage a countercampaign to the blind-man's-bluff insurgency where the enemy is rarely seen. The interservice-staffed SOG teams encountered their headwinds mostly from Washington departments and the conventional military set. They became a political football in the trimural contest among the Pentagon, State Department, and White House contestants. The wrangling amid the nation's bureaucracies was one hallmark of the Vietnam War that seemed destined to repeat itself.

Ground-level friction also existed between SOF and regular Army units, which the special operations troops sometimes aggravated by loose talk and nonregulation behavior, such as growing long hair, carrying foreign firearms, and wearing large brass Montagnard arm bracelets, which the highland dwellers appreciated. Rubbing the conventional military the wrong way persisted after the Vietnam War, nearly turning special operators into pariahs. The shadow warriors relished and promoted their antiestablishment conduct, which did not endear them to their mainstream comrades, who sometimes referred to Special Forces as "snake eaters" for their jungle survival skills.[34] But when it came to the SOF-CIA relationship, the interservice rivalries mattered little to most intelligence officers, who dressed in civilian clothes and wore their hair longer than the closely cropped Prussian army haircuts of the standard military. The Agency officers' orientation was different from general-purpose soldiers, and so was that of special operations fighters. Thus, they often bonded without the antagonism so characteristic of regular military services. But as things turned out, the asymmetries between special warfighters and line units proved of less concern than budgets, as shown below.

The collapse and surrender of South Vietnam resulted in an inward turn within the American body politic. Even though America's armed forces pulled out of Vietnam two years before the North's conventional invasion, the news media, academics, and political elites laid the blame for the outcome at the U.S. military's feet. Saigon's rout also induced a fall in popular support for the armed forces and a decline in military morale. The Vietnam War's end also led to severe defense spending cuts and the return of conventional thinking about America's international challenges. Resolved to never again step onto the "slippery slope" toward another rural insurgency, the Pentagon turned back to the reassuring familiar pattern of state-on-state industrial warfare aimed primarily at the Soviet Union in Europe.

The political and budgetary fallout impacted the Central Intelligence Agency and the Special Operations Forces, as well as the conventional military forces. The 1970s became known for the "hollow Army," as Edward C. Meyer, chairman of the Joint Chiefs, famously stated. The special forces groups suffered even more than line units during the budget contractions. The top brass deemed them expendable, even unnecessary, for the next war, which was sure to be clashes between armor columns and infantry divisions in the European theater. Funding for SOF fell to one-tenth of 1 percent of the entire defense budget, after its funds were cut by 95 percent.[35] The Green Beret detachments shrunk in number and in skills as training funds vanished. Other units faced extinction. Overall, Special Operations Forces hunkered down, awaiting a better day.

Congressionally mandated defense reductions compelled General Meyer to preside over reductions in forces and decreased armaments. But he did oversee an expansion in the SOF ranks by encouraging U.S. Army colonel Charles Beckwith to establish a new super-secret group designated the First Special Forces Operational Detachment–Delta, but popularly known as Delta Force, which was designed for hostage rescue and other counter-terrorism missions.[36] Based in part on the British Special Air Service concept, Beckwith's ultra-secret commandos were barely formed when they participated in the star-crossed Operation Eagle Claw to free fifty-two American hostages seized from the U.S. Embassy in Tehran in 1979. Because of mechanical break-downs in the mission helicopters and myriad other problems, Beckwith aborted the complex rescue enterprise.[37] The Desert One humiliation did result in another significant development in the SOF armory. The postmortem analysis of the dismal helicopter failures led to the formation of a dedicated air arm for special operations missions—the 160th Special Operations Aviation Regiment. It provided specialized air service to transport SOF teams to their targets as well as fire support for ground units. Lean budgets, therefore, fell short of completely curtailing necessary developments for enhancing future SOF capabilities.

The Post-Vietnam CIA and Iranian Hostage Debacle

The Agency thread of this SOF-CIA study must be interwoven into the events leading up to the failed Iranian hostage expedition. Emblematic of the post-Vietnam period was the investigation of the CIA conducted by the U.S. Senate Intelligence Committee under the leadership of Idaho senator Frank Church. Church characterized the CIA as a "rogue elephant."[38] His Senate hearings did much to expose some excesses, but they also debilitated the Agency's operations side for decades. Senator Church's revelations contributed to the withering of the spy agency's paramilitary functions and to its risk-aversion psychology that haunted many spymasters until the September 11 attacks.

During Jimmy Carter's presidency, Langley cut substantial numbers of its undercover operatives from the clandestine service. Several factors explain the downsizing within the Directorate of Operations. Carter and his CIA director, Stansfield Turner, reckoned that field officers and their support staffs were no longer needed after Vietnam. Turner and his top lieutenants gravitated toward the Directorate of Intelligence, which gathered intelligence, analyzed information, and drew assessments for Washington policy makers. On Turner's watch, the CIA cut some eight hundred Directorate of Operations personnel within a short period during 1979 in a purge that became known as the "Halloween Massacre."[39] Later, in a memoir, Turner reflected a change of heart: "In retrospect, I probably should not have effected the reductions of 820 positions at all, and certainly not the last 17."[40]

Moreover, the clandestine service underwent a rapid turnover in chiefs, which further depressed morale among the depleted ranks of paramilitary and agent-handling officers who worked with SOF in the late 1970s. Budget cutbacks after the Soviet

Union's collapse in 1991 likewise took a heavy toll on the intelligence community. America's 1990s replayed the follies of the 1920s by disarming and ignoring the emerging terrorist threats. Tellingly, the gutting of the Agency's operatives weakened its capabilities to mount the sorts of activities necessary in the post–Cold War era. All these cutbacks diminished U.S. defenses against terrorism. After the 9/11 attacks, the investigating National Commission on Terrorists Attacks pointed out the damage done to the spy service and its covert operations because of egregious decisions made years earlier that exposed the nation to terrorism.[41] Well before that judgment of history, CIA and SOF cooperation hit a bump in the road, according to the biographer of Army major Richard Meadows, a Special Forces legend. When the Iranian "students" stormed the U.S. Embassy in Tehran, the CIA pulled its case officers from Iran and stated that it had no assets within the country to assist the Pentagon's covert rescue mission. At a later date, Langley did put forward a retired agent, who was of Iranian descent; he managed, however, to cross swords with Colonel Beckwith. The American commander naturally lamented the fact that his Delta Force teams were proceeding into Iran "without accurate and timely intelligence."[42] Learning of his former military comrades' difficulties in what was seen as CIA obstruction, Meadows (who had already left military service) volunteered to go into Tehran to scout out the city and make local preparations for the hostage-rescue operation.

The CIA was cool to the military's plans. Nor did the Agency support Meadows's proposal to undertake a high-risk reconnaissance and coordination role to assist the hostage-rescue enterprise. Reluctantly, it offered some basic spy tradecraft training for Meadows and a false passport. A few active-duty Special Forces members from a team based in West Germany joined

Meadows in an undercover cell to do what CIA officers normally do in paramilitary operations. Therefore, the mission went forward. All of the Meadows team dressed in civilian clothes and entered the country illegally under false passports.[43] Their mission demonstrated extraordinary courage and resourcefulness to set foot in the belly of the fervidly anti-American state. They all made it safely out of Iran after the failure of the rescue mission.

In the end, the entire rescue enterprise came to grief. Two helicopter failures proved to be the Achilles' heel of the complex operation. Suspicions, nevertheless, lingered long after among SOF that the CIA had let down the military rescue operation. Subsequent revelations about the CIA's reluctant sharing of information fueled the wariness of the Agency within the special operations community.[44] Many years later, General Stanley McChrystal made reference to the low point in SOF-CIA relations at the time of Operation Eagle Claw in his memoir about Iraq and Afghanistan. Specifically, McChrystal lamented that at the time he formed the Joint Interagency Task Force (JIATF) in 2003, special operations personnel and CIA officers cooperated just slightly better than in the lead-up to Operation Eagle Claw.[45] The Delta Force's failed hostage rescue in Iran thus marked a nadir in the SOF-CIA nexus.

Nevertheless, defeat, or at least a major setback, can generate innovation and change in a manner that victory rarely does. And the Iranian hostage disgrace spawned a new intelligence agency and a new organizational architecture, as will be seen in the next chapter.

chapter four

The Emergence of a New Security Architecture

THE BOTCHED RESCUE RAID in the Iranian desert led the Pentagon to reassess its dependency on the CIA, which, as noted in the last chapter, it held partly responsible for the deficiencies in information about Iran and its government. In the aftermath of Eagle Claw, the Department of Defense complained about the inability to dispatch its own personnel to foreign soil for reconnaissance and intelligence purposes. The more narrowly focused Defense Intelligence Agency (DIA), founded in 1961, saw its primary mission as gathering battlefield information in support of tactical combat actions. But it was out of the action in Iran, having no authority to operate inside the country. In laying plans for a second hostage-rescue expedition, the Joint Chiefs of Staff moved to form a new Pentagon intelligence unit to lessen reliance on the CIA. This second operation never saw the light of day, as Iran released the fifty-two captured Americans during the presidential inauguration of Ronald Reagan in January 1981. But the Pentagon's Intelligence Support Activity (ISA) did materialize later the same year. Over the years, the ISA assumed several names, including "the Activity," Gray Fox, Task Force Orange, and the Army of Northern Virginia, for its headquarters at Fort Belvoir in Virginia. Whatever its name, it eventually supported SOF alone, particularly for short-term intelligence that required a close-in presence to adversaries.

The ISA, housed within the Department of Defense, was tantamount to the military's coming of age in a new era. Even before Nathan Hale broke with his officer peers to spy on the British, most armed forces resisted spying. Many soldiers thought snooping was beneath the honorable profession of arms. Terrorism and asymmetric tactics, however, required adaptation by military forces. The need for human observers to spy for the military proved to be essential in light of the failed Eagle Claw operation. From a small staff of fifty individuals, the ISA rapidly grew in personnel, budget, and ambition.

Unfortunately for the Activity, it became entangled in a series of amateurish rogue plots to rescue phantom American prisoners of war in Southeast Asia during the 1980s. The Activity's naïve shenanigans embarrassed both the top military brass and civilian officials at the Department of Defense during the early Reagan years. Those problems marginalized the ISA during the Grenada intervention. Its rival, the CIA, capitalized on the reports about an out-of-control ISA. The Agency did all it could to undermine and confound its human-spying competitor. As a consequence, the CIA's actions did little to win over the ISA or the Pentagon to its side in the competitive world of Washington politics.[1] The Pentagon-CIA animosity, long a feature of the Washington political scene, intensified from the 1980s. Chastened by its mistakes, the Activity survived its growing pains and lived on to perform herculean human and signals intelligence missions after the September 11 attacks, as will be discussed later.

The 1980s also recorded a sweeping overhaul of the command structure for the Special Operations Forces. In the aftermath of the frustrating Operation Eagle Claw, the Joint Special Operations Command (JSOC) was established, in part, on the recommendation of Colonel Beckwith to the Joint Chiefs of Staff to ensure coordination, synchronization, and interoperability for the planning and execution of special operations missions. Half a decade later, Congress enacted legislation that established the U.S. Special Operations Command (USSOCOM) under a four-star officer and a separate, dedicated budget. Organizationally, JSOC is a subunified command under the parent USSOCOM, but JSOC functioned as the immediate nerve cell and action arm for special operations strikes and related missions. The U.S. Special Operations Command came about through the efforts of Senators Sam Nunn (Georgia) and William Cohen (Maine). Their legislative cooperation, the Nunn-Cohen Amendment, an amendment to the broader Pentagon reorganization in the Goldwater-Nichols Department of Defense Reorganization Act (Senator Barry Goldwater and Representative William "Bill" Nichols), ironed out a number of issues.[2]

Whereas the overall Goldwater-Nichols collaboration concentrated on regional combatant commanders and interservice cooperation, the Nunn-Cohen Amendment zeroed in on issues that confronted SOF. It gave them their own command and budget. The amendment also specified USSOCOM's oversight over active and reserve SOF within the United States and beyond. In addition, it established an assistant secretary of defense for special operations and low-intensity conflicts (known as ASD/SOLIC inside the Pentagon). Finally, it defined SOF missions as those that encompassed unconventional warfare, reconnaissance, direct action, counterproliferation of weapons of mass destruction, counterterrorism, foreign internal defense, psychological operations, and other assignments requested by the secretary of defense and the president.[3] A congressional mandate established USSOCOM, but it took Washington's prodding to activate the new command in Tampa, Florida, and to get the services to assign specialized units to the new command. Even before the closing of the Cold War era, SOF saw a lot of action around the globe.

Grenada, Panama, and the Persian Gulf War: Parallel Lines Meet

During the U.S. Grenada and Panama interventions, Special Operations Forces were employed only in support missions to the overall military offensive. They engaged in direct actions against enemy personnel and conducted reconnaissance operations for combat intelligence that was useful for the larger military effort. For its part, the Central Intelligence Agency in each of these brief operations supplied intelligence, which SOF consumed for tactical information about its adversary's strength and location. Military forces rely on intelligence from a variety of sources—satellite, electronic eavesdropping, photo reconnaissance, and human sources—to perform their missions. In short, the CIA served as another conduit of information. It also made assessments of America's peer adversaries' capabilities and intentions. The same pattern held during the Persian Gulf War, which was also of relatively short duration and fought largely along conventional military lines. The close interaction between special operators and undercover field officers, so characteristic of paramilitary operations or insurgencies, is limited in regular fire-and-maneuver conflicts. So, while the eyes, ears, and daggers of America's security arms interacted, their "jointness" never enfolded them into each other's organizational fabric in the way the Vietnamese insurgency or the future counterterrorism campaigns did.

Before the onset of the Persian Gulf War in early 1991, Major General Wayne Downing, the head of JSOC, worked with the CIA on plans to rescue American diplomats trapped in the

Kuwait City embassy when Iraq's forces overran the small kingdom in August 1990. The plans came to naught because Saddam Hussein released the captives. Downing also worked up plans with the Agency to capture the Iraqi dictator. The plans were rejected. Neither the commander of the U.S. Central Command (CENTCOM), General Norman Schwarzkopf, nor the chairman of the JCS, Colin Powell, desired any high-risk ventures to derail either the diplomatic efforts to resolve the Iraqis' occupation of Kuwait or the accelerating military buildup in the region if diplomacy failed.[4] The SOF-CIA planning, nonetheless, was a foreshadowing of later warrior-spy operations against high-value targets.

Moreover, General Schwarzkopf was less than enamored with "snake eaters." Concerned about provoking the Iraqis to strike during the massive military build-up phase before the start of the ground offensive, Schwarzkopf repeatedly reined in SOF plans for commando raids and deep-penetration reconnaissance. After the war, he reminisced: "I did not want a bunch of guys running 'Rambo-type' operations and have to divert forces from the real war to bail them out."[5] That objection aside, the overall commander of the Gulf War did ultimately employ SOF in operational feints, reconnaissance, and direct-action missions in support of the main conventional offensive.[6]

At the start of the land war, Schwarzkopf deployed Navy SEALs to bluff Hussein into thinking that the main American thrust was planned for Kuwait's beaches. A dozen SEALs strung a line of buoys identical to those used to mark amphibious landings zones. Other special operators seized oil platforms in the Gulf. The commanding general also dispatched ten Special Forces teams deep behind Iraqi lines for reconnaissance purposes. Special operations teams were also widely dispersed to hunt for and neutralize Iraqi scud missile batteries based in

Iraq's western expanse of desert. These and related swashbuckling-type military engagements were always subordinate to the main heavy armored thrusts to liberate Kuwait from Hussein's army of occupation, however.

Prior to the start of the Gulf War, the SOF and CIA teamed up to hatch plans, some of which foreshadowed their celebrated partnership in eliminating terrorists after the 9/11 attacks. General Downing worked with CIA officials to either ambush or capture senior members of Iraq's leadership, including the chief of the security police, who was the president's half-brother, and even Saddam Hussein himself. Generals Schwarzkopf and Powell nixed these plots, too.[7]

Blocked from cloak-and-dagger actions, the SOF commanders did something worthy of emulation and duplication in light of the planned terrorist assault on the U.S. consulate in Benghazi, Libya, on September 11, 2012, during which Washington's ambassador and three other Americans were killed. In 1990, the two special operations generals took preemptive steps to protect American embassies from potential assaults by Saddam Hussein. General Downing and General Carl Steiner (commander of the U.S. Special Operations Command in Tampa) persuaded the Pentagon to position SOF forces overseas so they could respond to any possible Iraqi terrorism. The CIA supplied intelligence. Some special warfare operators were inserted within embassies that appeared particularly vulnerable to terrorism. Other civilian-attired operators shadowed suspected Iraqi agents. Next, the SOF generals deployed more than a dozen helicopters and commando squads to Great Britain in order to have enough counterterrorism muscle on hand to respond to three separate, simultaneous terrorist incidents in Europe or the Middle East.[8] It was farseeing and prudent preparation for a possible terrorist eventuality worthy of repeated emulation.

Formative Actions in Panama, Colombia, Somalia, and the Balkans

The 1990s were not barren of SOF-CIA cooperation. Indeed, the Joint Special Operations Command developed its manhunting skills first acquired and tested in Panama, Colombia, Somalia, and the Balkans. And the CIA fine-tuned its intelligence gathering and detective work to locate desperados on the lam. The 1990s, in fact, witnessed the coalescing of these two communities in search operations. For the Panama intervention, JSOC picked up the mission of finding and apprehending Manuel Noriega, who went into hiding as U.S. forces descended on the Central American country. Delta Force and SEAL Team 6 elements (both designated in the category of the elite special mission units, or SMU) spent frustrating days searching for the Panamanian dictator. The chase turned out to be a useful precursor of what special mission units undertook against insurgent terrorists later in Afghanistan and Iraq. In this initial tracking job, the trail went cold just before Noriega surfaced in the Vatican's embassy in Panama, where he surrendered to the U.S. forces.

The Joint Special Operations Command gained more experience in tracking down fugitives when it was called on in mid-1992 to aid in the pursuit of Pablo Escobar, the notorious Colombian drug kingpin. About a dozen Delta and SEAL Team 6 operatives rotated into and out of Bogota and Medellín for more than a year. Theirs was officially a training mission of Colombia's "Search Bloc"—the local forces going after Escobar and his henchmen. But the special operator shooters often joined their trainees in some sweeps. At the end of 1993, Search Bloc forces uncovered Escobar's hideout when he spoke too long on the phone, permitting his location to be fixed. The ensuing shootout resulted in the death of the narcotics chieftain. The SOF contingent was ably assisted by the Intelligence Support

Activity, which mounted tracking equipment on two small civilian aircraft so as to zero in on Escobar's cell phone calls.[9] In the words of one of the authorities, tracking down Escobar would "have long-lasting impact on the command, as it provided a 'template' for how to use a quarry's cell phone to track him down." This method was widely adopted a decade later against many terrorist figures from Mindanao to Mazar-i-Sharif.[10]

Not long before the conclusion of the SOF mission in Colombia, Delta operatives and Army Rangers encountered a pitched gun battle in the dusty streets of Mogadishu, the capital of Somalia, in pursuit of another elusive man at large. In the twilight of his presidency, George H. W. Bush sent more than twenty thousand U.S. troops into Somalia to distribute food to a population suffering from starvation because of clan and warlord clashes. Following the turnover of the American food relief effort to the United Nations in May 1993, the Bill Clinton administration stepped up military ventures to restore order to the desperately poor Horn of Africa nation. Washington held vague notions of nation building in the deeply fractured Somalian society. The central antagonist to American plans was Mohamed Aidid, a clan chieftain, who murdered and intimidated rivals in the seaside city and environs. His attacks tossed Mogadishu into turmoil.

On October 3, 1993, a Ranger and Delta task force swooped into the center of Mogadishu on helicopters to capture two of Aidid's lieutenants. While the mission accomplished this objective, it ran into a mass counterattack in which two MH-60 Black Hawk helicopters were shot down, and eighteen servicemen were killed in the melee. Somali casualties are unknown but thought to be at least five hundred dead. The fifteen-hour firefight ended after an improvised rescue column from the nearby airport reached the embattled U.S. forces and spirited them to safety.[11] Despite seizing the Aidid deputies and displaying enormous courage under withering fire from street corners, windows, and alleys, the U.S. force suffered a blow to its prestige from international condemnation. Internally, the Clinton White House looked flummoxed by what had been a humanitarian project gone terribly awry. JSOC, nonetheless, learned valuable lessons for future raids for snatching prey.[12]

It was in the Balkans where JSOC and the CIA honed their manhunting expertise so valued in the post-9/11 counterterrorist campaign. Atrocities and crimes against humanity marked the Balkans war, which concluded after negotiations in Dayton, Ohio, in late 1995. The Dayton Peace Accords included stipulations that war criminals must be charged before the International Criminal Tribunal for the former Yugoslavia at The Hague in the Netherlands. Those fearing prosecution, mostly Serbs, went into hiding when the tribunal issued arrest warrants. Because the Western powers divided Bosnia into American, British, and French sectors, the jurisdictional quandaries perplexed the outsider nations. If indicted figures went to ground in the U.S. sector, then JSOC and the CIA got the job to arrest them. When the U.S. intelligence collectors located a suspect in another sector, the American authorities notified the other command of an impending snatch mission.

The SOF teams used unmanned aerial vehicles (the RQ-11A and RQ-11B Raven), which were the size of model airplanes, for surveillance of their target before striking to minimize or eliminate potential "showstoppers," or obstacles. On other occasions, the snatch teams used secret electronic systems similar to those used to track Pablo Escobar's cell phone calls to pinpoint his physical location. Experts from the National Security Agency (NSA), the super-secret eavesdropping service at Fort Meade, joined their counterparts from the SOF, ISA, and CIA in teams to trace the whereabouts of the accused mass murderers. NSA's signals collection and processing mastery enabled monitoring of suspects' locations. Once the accused were found, Delta or Team 6 personnel painstakingly rehearsed their take-down techniques for fugitives to avoid mishaps.[13]

The joint pursuit of indicted individuals also reinforced the partnership between JSOC operators and Agency operatives that became all-important half a decade later. The liaison often took place between the CIA's Special Activities Division (SAD), where SOF often placed a military officer to serve as deputy chief of the SAD. At this early stage of cooperation between the two communities, the CIA worked to locate the fugitives, and JSOC executed the raids to apprehend them. During the dragnets for fleeing individuals, SOF improved their intelligence-gathering skills and experimented with technical tracking devices. But the command itself worked closely with the Agency in ad hoc teams that were a forerunner to the fusion cells in Iraq and Afghanistan. Special operators, CIA officers, ISA personnel, and NSA technicians worked alongside each other because no one entity possessed the wherewithal to locate and subdue the designated targets, who hid out among their loyal compatriots. It could have been the proverbial search for a needle in a haystack, but advanced technology, shared expertise, and hard work netted all the big fish. The biggest payoff, nevertheless, stemmed from the forging of professional and personal relationships between the special mission units and the CIA's Special Activities Division.[14]

The rest of the 1990s marked the Pentagon's reluctance to get into the fight against the growing al Qaeda terrorist threat. If anything, America's top brass regarded terrorism as a distraction from large land-unit warfare. Besides, they believed that it was the CIA's job to handle terrorist threats. During President Clinton's first term, the Department of Defense shied away from covert operations. It wanted to fight big conflicts like the Persian

Gulf War. The SOF operations in Somalia just deepened skepticism among the Pentagon chiefs about special warriors. What went wrong in the Mogadishu "Black Hawk Down" crisis offered a cautionary tale for SOF troops caught up in an exploding powder magazine of seething anti-American hatred. The bloody incident made the Joint Chiefs of Staff risk averse to limited missions involving the special operations community until the 9/11 terrorist attacks.

Throughout the balance of the 1990s, the top Pentagon brass resisted calls from the president's Counterterrorism Security Group, chaired by the indefatigable Richard Clarke, to eliminate Osama bin Laden by cruise missile or SOF attack.[15] The SOF command was eager to deploy special operators against the terrorist impresario but was never given the green light, as outlined in the *9/11 Commission Report*.[16] Instead, the military chiefs decried what they claimed was inadequate "actionable intelligence" to trigger a SOF assault against the al Qaeda head. This frustrated General Peter Schoomaker, who commanded USSOCOM in the late 1990s. Later he vented: "It was like having a brand new Ferrari in the garage, and nobody wants to race it because you might dent the fender."[17] Fearing another Battle of Mogadishu, General Hugh Shelton, the JCS chairman, put forward elaborate plans replete with large bodies of standby forces for rescue of the SOF operators just in case things on the ground went amiss. Rather than commando strikes, the plans resembled small-scale invasions. Faced with these prodigious operational plans, the Clinton White House backed off and did nothing.[18]

Just as Sherlock Holmes took note of the dog that did not bark to solve a mystery, a student of these behind-the-scenes counterterrorism deliberations must call out the glaring absence of close SOF-CIA interaction against the jihadi threat. Nowhere in the accounts of policy makers considering strikes on Osama bin

Laden before he struck the Twin Towers can there be found the tight engagement between special warfighters and intelligence professionals so characteristic of the next decade. So, while blame is cast on the U.S. security apparatus for failing to neutralize Osama bin Laden either by capture or by gunfire, it is important to underscore the key missing variable of SOF-CIA integration. Years later, their coordination enabled an effective instrument to be forged against the Taliban, al Qaeda, and other networks, as will be detailed.

Even the notion of providing aid to the Northern Alliance, the anti-Taliban front in Afghanistan, encountered the opposition from the Joint Staff (which serves the JCS).[19] The task fell to the CIA to maintain a trickle of assistance to the beleaguered Northern Alliance until the al Qaeda "planes operation" called for turning it into a virtual ally. The Pentagon's preference and posture for regular battlefields left it unready for a fast-moving intervention against the Taliban regime, which hosted al Qaeda. Instead, the CIA took the lead in America's counterattack.

During the later 1990s, the Pentagon also demonstrated caution about wading into a messy land engagement in northern Iraq after the Persian Gulf War. Rather, the United States, Britain, and, for a time, France dominated the airspace over northern and southern Iraq in the wake of Saddam Hussein's ruthless suppression of his antiregime opponents. In the north, among the mainly Kurdish population, the overhead no-fly zone enforced by the three Western air forces allowed a measure of autonomy to take root. The CIA sent field officers to work among the Kurds, and the Pentagon also dispatched a small number of lightly armed troops in Operation Provide Comfort. The Joint Chiefs rejected CIA requests for assistance in covert operations to overthrow Hussein either from bases in Kurdistan or from a coterie of disgruntled Sunni generals.[20] In the end, the Clinton White

House pulled the plug on the coup plans in Iraq, fearing a reprise of the Bay of Pigs fiasco with Cuban exiles.[21]

Despite the Pentagon's hesitancy, however, its Middle East command began a new track to deal with potential terrorist attacks. Like the biblical mustard seed that blossomed, there existed one budding initiative that pointed toward closer SOF-CIA collaboration in the fight against jihadi terrorism. Within the COMSOCCENT (the special operations component within the U.S. Central Command) before hijacked planes hit the World Trade Center, a crisis response team (CRT) took shape to strike in reaction to or to hit preemptively against terrorists. General Tommy Franks backed the CRT's formation. When briefed, Director of Central Intelligence George Tenet was enthusiastic about it because the CRT gave the CIA an in-house "door-kicking" capability, thereby sparing it a dependence on unreliable host-nation forces in the wake of the terrorist bombing of the USS *Cole* in a Yemeni harbor.[22] The spy agency saw in the CRT an answer to its need for a counterstrike unit. The full measure of this evolving joint strike-force concept burst dramatically in the media with the raid on Osama bin Laden, although that mission was preceded by countless SOF-CIA operations in Iraq and Afghanistan, as shown in the next chapter.

chapter five

September 11th and the Integration of Special Operators and Intelligence Officers

THE SEPTEMBER 11TH TERRORISM, U.S. interventions into Afghanistan and Iraq, and the intensifying campaign against jihadi violence—all vaulted the JSOC and CIA onto center stage of the nation's security. In time, these activities also tightened the alignment between the military's special operators and CIA case officers far closer than in any previous time. Just as it is often said that necessity is the mother of invention, the campaign against terrorism was the catalyst for an alliance. When al Qaeda jihadis crashed commercial jets into the World Trade Center and the Pentagon on September 11, 2001, the calamity enabled Secretary of Defense Donald Rumsfeld to propel SOF to the vanguard of the counterassault on what then was termed "the global war on terror." He brought out of retirement SOF general Peter Schoomaker to head the U.S. Army as its chief of staff, which was widely interpreted as a symbolic turn toward special operations forces. Other far-reaching actions prepared SOF to confront the globalizing terrorist threat, which will be subsequently sketched.

The coalescing of the military and intelligence communities gave rise to an often-confusing debate about the statutory authorities that governed the way the Joint Special Operation Command (along with the whole defense community) and the CIA operated. JSOC and the Pentagon itself operate under Title 10 of the U.S. Code for the armed forces. Title 10 does not exclude the military from covert operations. Moreover, the secretary of defense possesses authority under Title 50 of the U.S. Code to collect intelligence and mount covert actions. The CIA's authority also derives from Title 50, which permits it to run clandestine and covert operations at the ultimate discretion of the president. It operates under congressional oversight in that two of its committees can hold hearings—the Senate Select Committee on Intelligence and the House Permanent Select Committee on Intelligence.[1] One journalist viewed this reporting relationship as empowering JSOC to operate around the world "with less accountability than the CIA."[2] The reality is much more complex. Congressional oversight of the Department of Defense is exercised by Senate and House Armed Service Committees. Thus JSOC, along with the larger military, is required to brief congressional committees. The armed forces, therefore, do not have free reign to operate without accountability to Capitol Hill. Still, the legislative scrutiny of military clandestine operations has historically been much less intense than those covert actions conducted by the CIA, primarily because the former operations are conducted within a traditional structure.

In reality, Title 50 leaves the president the choice of agency for covert operations, which affords the U.S. government some thin plausible deniability about overseas undercover activity. In reality, the knowledge of these types of shadowy operations and their real authors is often an open secret. America's hand, for example, in the CIA-aided coup in 1954 Guatemala was known almost immediately afterward. The president can authorize the Pentagon as well as the CIA to carry out off-the-books missions so long as that individual designates the action as necessary for the national interest and identifies the agency—CIA or Defense Department—responsible for conducting and funding the mission. Using the CIA cover in a quasi-military action, such as the Navy SEAL raid to remove Osama bin Laden, amounted to a course far less than actual war, at least from the American statutory perspective.

Had a formal de jure military force been used to cross the border and eliminate Osama bin Laden instead, such an overt intervention would have been seen as an act of war because the force invaded Pakistan's sovereignty. A country other than Pakistan in all likelihood would not even have tolerated an attack on its soil by a slightly below-the-radar force operating under the transparent artifice of its own codes specifying a secret-mission designation. As it was, thousands of Pakistanis took to the streets with anti-American protests in the wake of the SEALs' helicopter raid. As for the Islamabad government, it often played a delicate, complex game of closing its eyes to some American offenses, such as the drone strikes on militants, when it gained tangible rewards for its forbearance. For many years, the United States provided substantial material and military aid to Pakistan. Furthermore, some drone missiles killed militants who were also in the Pakistani crosshairs. Therefore, Islamabad greeted their deaths with a sense of relief rather than anger at Washington. The return of Nawaz Sharif to the office of prime minister in June 2013 at first augured a cancellation in Pakistan's policy of turning a blind eye to U.S. air strikes on its territory, though. As a candidate, he criticized America's drone policy. Once in office, however, he followed in the footsteps of his predecessors and, indeed, widened ground attacks on Islamist militants in the country's turbulent tribal belt. Thus, the Pakistani piece of the mosaic formed an important dimension to the implementation of America's statutory codes for waging covert actions. In brief, the South Asian country went along with Washington's clandestine drone strategy against declared terrorist targets within its territory.

The ambiguity between the two authorities is not as much a legal issue as an operational and policy one. One legal expert avowed that "confusion over Title 10 and Title 50 has more to do with congressional oversight and its attendant internecine power struggles than with operational or statutory authorities." In his words, the problem stems from "Congress's stovepiped view of national security operations . . . [which is] operationally dangerous because it creates concerns about interagency cooperation at exactly the time in history when our policy and legal structures should be encouraging increased interagency coordination and cooperation against interconnected national security threats." Subsequently, he concluded that "Congress could end the Title 10–Title 50 debate by simply reforming its oversight of military and intelligence activities and align oversight with the statutory authorities."[3] The confusion should not extend to the fact that SOF and CIA operators possess dual lines of authority. Nor does it appear to have erected hurdles for the actual operators in their missions. The Title 10–Title 50 discussion resurfaced during President Obama's second term in the guise of returning the CIA to its traditional spying mission by moving away from paramilitary and kinetic operations, which will be mentioned later in these pages.

The Afghan Prelude to the SOF-CIA Fusion

During the quarter century before the 9/11 attacks, the Central Intelligence Agency lined up behind the mujahedin resistance to the Soviet Union's invasion of Afghanistan. Indeed, CIA field officers moved into the mountainous country from their base within the U.S. embassy in Pakistan well before Moscow's dispatch of the Red Army to prop up its beleaguered strongman in Kabul in late 1979. These CIA case officers established contact with tribal leaders who opposed the Kremlin's spreading Communist political and secular influence. Washington, in fact, had shown geostrategic interest in Afghanistan during the early Cold War, when it competed with Moscow for leverage by constructing irrigation canals and the large Kandahar airport as a fuel stopover between the Middle East and India before long-distance jets bypassed it. With abundant historical irony, the airport years later accommodated U.S. warplanes in the American-led NATO intervention against the Taliban. Before the Soviet military incursion, CIA operatives recruited and funded Afghans who resented the Soviet sway over the Kabul government. As for the Kremlin, it aimed to backstop the wobbly Marxist regime's efforts to secure its hold on a restive population. In the months leading up to the Red Army dispatching paratroops and *Spetsnaz* (Russian acronym for special purpose forces), the CIA personnel cultivated several assets within the future mujahedin ranks and furnished cash as well as small amounts of humanitarian assistance.

With the Kremlin's dramatic military invasion on Christmas Eve 1979, Afghanistan leapt onto Washington policy makers' radar screens. President Jimmy Carter began modest shipments of military equipment and outdated rifles to aid the mujahedin resistance to a brutal Soviet occupation. His successor, Ronald Reagan, stepped up the flow of weaponry and cash to the Afghans through Pakistani military and intelligence channels. The CIA stood front and center in this large-scale paramilitary operation that entailed arming, training, and intelligence transfers. Reagan's strategy to sap Soviet economic strength by a protracted Afghan struggle paid off by the mid-1980s. The bleeding Afghanistan ulcer convinced the new Soviet ruler, Mikhail Gorbachev, to cut the USSR's losses and retreat from the war. The last Red Army troops pulled out in February 1989. America's hand, and that of the CIA, in the Soviet defeat was extensive. This lengthy Afghan experience positioned the CIA to assume a leading role in the planning and execution of the U.S. ground intervention into the rugged Central Asian country a little more than a decade later as the Twin Towers and Pentagon still smoldered.

Before that SOF- and CIA-led attack into Afghanistan, the Agency underwent a profound reorientation. The disintegration of the Soviet Union in 1991 removed America's arch-nemesis after a four-decade preoccupation by Langley. In fact, as noted in chapter 2, the founding of the CIA stemmed directly from the Soviet menace after World War II. While post–Cold War Russia still possessed a devastating nuclear capacity, it no longer threatened the United States in a global confrontation. The expiration of the Cold War lessened the need for an American intelligence apparatus aimed at discerning what Red Square was doing and planning. The Pentagon also experienced an anticlimax to the Cold War, but its military forces found employment in a string of interventions in Panama, Iraq, Somalia, Bosnia, and Kosovo before the terrorist "planes operation" hit America's military and financial symbols, killing nearly three thousand people.

As the lethal terrorist incidents mounted during the 1990s, the Central Intelligence Agency retooled to tackle the elusive threat posed by Osama bin Laden. It founded a bin Laden unit in 1995—the first time it created a "station" focused on one individual. Headed by Michael Scheuer and staffed with Arabic-fluent experts on the Middle East and Islamic thought, it initiated a manhunt, which took a decade and a half to get its man. Although the unit, together with the Clinton administration's National

Security Council and the Defense Department, missed or canceled operations to kill or capture bin Laden several times, it did build up a network of dissident Afghans who opposed the Taliban regime for its granting safe haven to al Qaeda militants. These CIA assets turned out to be of considerable assistance to the future SOF-CIA intervention against the terrorist-harboring Taliban regime.[4]

Days after the al Qaeda–hijacked commercial jets crashed into the World Trade Center, Pentagon, and a Pennsylvania field, President George W. Bush demanded a counterattack strategy against the terrorist havens in Afghanistan. Rather than the Pentagon offering up a ready-to-execute assault plan, it was the Central Intelligence Agency that presented one. The Department of Defense wanted six months to position forces and matériel for a conventional invasion. At the White House on September 13 and elaborated two days later at Camp David, the CIA director, George Tenet, outlined the blueprint for what soon took place inside Afghanistan. Memorably, the nation's top spy stressed: "We would be the insurgents" against an unpopular sitting Taliban regime.[5] By this reference, the CIA spymaster meant the United States would participate in and aid an antigovernment insurgency rather than assume Washington's traditional role of propping up an embattled regime under siege by guerrillas in the countryside, as happened in South Vietnam, Bolivia, and El Salvador during the Cold War.

Tenet called for the deployment of CIA paramilitary teams to connect with anti-Taliban militias and warlords. Joined by Special Forces, these teams would harness and empower resistance groups, notably the Northern Alliance, to topple the Taliban regime, which protected Osama bin Laden and the al Qaeda network. The CIA counterterrorism chief, Cofer Black, added detail in a PowerPoint presentation of the Agency's proposal.

Composed of Tajiks, Uzbek, Hazara, and other non-Pashtun fighters, the Northern Alliance had been at war with the largely Pashtun-populated Taliban movement since 1996, when the Taliban militia swept into power in Kabul.[6] Occupying a sliver of territory in the Panjshir Valley northeast of Kabul, the Northern Alliance received assistance from India, Iran, and Russia as well as the United States. All these powers harbored apprehensions about what Taliban rule held for their respective national interests in Central Asia.

The CIA's plan of attack struck the White House as innovative because it was, appealingly, implementable in just weeks. The blueprint, nevertheless, was classic OSS-CIA clandestine action—the use of intelligence, the insertion of paramilitary groups to team up with local forces, the application of air power, and the participation of lightly armed forces, in this case special operators. Refined and enhanced by USSOCOM, the CIA scheme formed the basis of the U.S. counterstrike against the Taliban regime and its al Qaeda guests three weeks after the Twin Towers attack. The Department of Defense contributed Operational Detachment Alpha teams, widely known as A-Teams or Special Forces, to link up with friendly Afghan militia commanders and to laser-in air strikes against the Taliban. In this latter duty, U.S. Air Force combat air controllers played a part too. As the scale of the operation escalated into a widespread land conflict, the CIA and Pentagon agreed that the command of field activities "would migrate over time from the CIA to Defense," a much larger department.[7] Hard on the heels of the insertion of CIA field operatives into the Panjshir basin, Special Forces troops entered the fray, coordinating with the local militias and lasering-in air strikes by U.S. Air Force and Navy warplanes.[8]

Coming in the wake of CIA–Special Forces infiltration was the active role of the Joint Special Operations Command, which inserted and coordinated U.S. Army Rangers, Navy SEALs, Delta Force, and Task Force Orange—the super-secret signals intelligence unit also known, as noted earlier, as the Intelligence Support Activity and Gray Fox. In time, these elements combined with the Central Intelligence Agency to form highly effective manhunting cells in Afghanistan and Iraq. Before these SOF deployments, the CIA headquarters in Langley placed a small SOF team within its Counterterrorism Center (CTC) to assist the Agency in planning its penetration into Afghanistan to establish contact with the anti-Taliban resistance. The CIA officials "welcomed the military trio warmly, making sure they had full access to everything the Agency was doing."[9]

Thus, the first to fight in Afghanistan were not the soldiers from the sea but rather CIA field officers in Operation Jawbreaker. They preceded all the U.S. military forces into the conflict against the Taliban. Journalists reported that the CIA's opening gambit provoked frustration within the Pentagon's E-Ring power corridor. Secretary of Defense Donald Rumsfeld displayed impatience at CIA paramilitary teams landing in Afghanistan prior to Special Forces. Be that as it may, the rivalrous feelings stayed relegated to the upper levels. One CIA official at the CTC expressed his displeasure with the "dysfunctional" Defense Department bureaucracy, which he viewed as rigid. Yet the same CIA official praised the Special Forces commander in the theater. He wrote that Colonel John Mulholland, the Special Forces Fifth Group commander in Uzbekistan, was "a great partner."[10]

Bob Woodward, a *Washington Post* correspondent, wrote in his book *Bush at War* about how the CIA's "Hank" (later identified as Henry Crumpton at the CIA's Counterterrorism Center) recognized the importance of getting right the integration of SOF operators and CIA field officers during the antiterrorist operation at the start of the Afghan counterattack. Woodward cites Hank communicating in a message to CIA field personnel saying, among other things, that "we are fighting for the future of CIA/DOD integrated counterterrorism warfare around the world." Acknowledging that "we will make mistakes as we chart new territory," Hank added that "our concept of partnership is sound."[11] In an insider's book, *Jawbreaker*, Hank is also reported as commenting to the Agency's field-level chief of the Afghanistan intervention: "We have to be married to CENTCOM." According to the same account, the CIA ground commander replied: "We fight together, or we die separately."[12] Such comments presaged the close SOF-CIA collaboration in the war on terror.

Early on in the first George W. Bush administration, the White House further eroded the distinctions separating SOF and the CIA, especially in paramilitary missions. This blurring of traditional lines resulted from an ad hoc process driven by operational exigencies rather than from a step-by-step road map executed from congressional legislation. But there were obstacles along the way. Voicing frustration with the CIA relationship, Secretary Rumsfeld repeatedly said to General Tommy Franks, the CENTCOM commander: "The Department of Defense is many times bigger than the CIA, and yet we are still here like little birds in a nest, waiting for someone to drop food in our mouths." He added: "It seems we couldn't do anything until the Agency gave us a morsel of intelligence or established the first links on the ground." Yet Rumsfeld also wrote in his memoir: "I worked as closely with CIA Director George Tenet as I have with any government official."[13] But the Pentagon civilian leadership regarded the Agency with disdain.

On the ground in Afghanistan a different, more cooperative relationship unfolded between spy and operator. CIA case officers fed target information from their own Predator drones to

JSOC, which used it to hunt down and kill Taliban resisters to the U.S. military footprint taking hold in the country. The Agency also lent its armed Predators to strike Taliban militias in vehicles or entrenched positions, because JSOC at this time lacked missile-equipped Predators. In early November 2001, just weeks after the SOF-CIA touchdown amid the Northern Alliance, the tables turned, and the CIA urgently needed JSOC assistance to rescue an important source in southern Afghanistan, whose life hung in the balance as Taliban fighters searched for his whereabouts. This individual was rallying his fellow Pashtun tribesmen against the Taliban, a certain death sentence. JSOC turned to one of its elite, and most secretive units, SEAL Team 6, often referred to by its bland cover name of the Naval Special Warfare Development Group (or DevGru) since 1989. Often, the plainer the designation in clandestine forces, the more exciting the unit. Another case in point is the highly direct-action Delta Force, which was referred to as the Combat Applications Group.

Although hard-pressed by demands for its helicopters, JSOC still dispatched two Black Hawks with SEAL Team 6 members to pluck the CIA source to safety. He was no run-of-the-mill CIA contact; he was Hamid Karzai, the future president of Afghanistan, whom Afghan watchers had long identified as someone who could lead the impoverished country toward the West. Two weeks later Team 6 special warriors safely returned Karzai to Kabul and served as his bodyguards for a time. Without suffering pangs of gratitude, Karzai later tried to shut down their nocturnal house searches as against Afghan customs but failed to halt them entirely.[14] At the Bonn conference in December, Karzai's fellow delegates chose the English-speaking Pashtun to be president. Karzai's rescue from his fellow Pashtun tribesmen, nonetheless, consolidated the budding alignment between the two security communities. As was so often true, events in the battle theaters brought together intelligence officials and special mission units despite the intramural rivalries playing out inside the Washington Beltway.

Secretary Rumsfeld went on to preside over a substantial growth in the Special Operations Forces' capacity. Its budget quadrupled from $2.3 billion in 2001 to more than $10 billion in the 2013 fiscal year, which still represented just 4 percent of the total base defense budget. This figure includes amounts contributed by the other military services in personnel and standard equipment. This means that SOCOM received assistance from the Air Force and Navy, such as transportation and logistical support, which counted as part of its financial budget. This fact makes understandable why SOCOM commanders point out their dependence on the other branches for assistance in their missions. Personnel figures also underwent similar swelling and stand now at more than 66,000, which comes to 5 percent of the Department of Defense total.[15]

The defense secretary also elevated SOCOM's standing to spearhead the global war on terror. At this stage of the global terror war, SOCOM lacked the ships, planes, and logistics to handle worldwide planning and execution of a counterterrorism campaign. In fact, Special Operations Forces were tied to the half-dozen regional combatant commanders (who had broad geographic zones of responsibility) for the conduct of operations within their respective command areas. Rumsfeld felt dissatisfied with the combatant commanders' likely performance in this new kind of warfare.[16] He wanted a much more agile force capable of no-notice operations to strike back at or to head off a terrorist attack. In time, SOCOM, and especially its sub-headquarters JSOC, fulfilled the Pentagon chief's priority for a lighter, faster-moving strike force with integrated intelligence. But when its time arrived, the CIA's Counterterrorism Center formed an integral part of the intelligence-driven fleet-footed unit. Complementing the Agency's assistance to JSOC was the Intelligence Support Activity, which Rumsfeld insisted be moved from the Army's control to JSOC. It took until 2004 to complete the two-year transfer, in the course of which it underwent a name change to Task Force Orange, or simply Orange.[17]

The post-9/11 anti-terror campaign also prompted Secretary Rumsfeld to assess the contours and strategies for special operators in combating terrorism. That process took two years. On September 16, 2003, Rumsfeld issued a far-reaching executive order that aimed to disrupt and destroy the al Qaeda network and its various facilitators in the undeclared war zones beyond Iraq and Afghanistan. Dubbed the EXORD or Al Qaeda Network Executive Order, it was the Pentagon's equivalent of a presidential finding, which the White House transmits to Congress when it authorizes the CIA to undertake covert actions. Hence, the Rumsfeld directive represented marching orders for the Joint Special Operations Command to hunt down al Qaeda elements in more than a dozen countries.[18] The CIA, under its Title 50 authority, needed to brief Congress, even if in closed sessions, to select members. JSOC avoided the same congressional oversight because it executed what were viewed as somewhat traditional military operations within an established military chain of command. The eighty-page EXORD listed some fifteen countries in which JSOC operations might take place to capture, kill, or spy. Under its authority, JSOC sent deep-cover operators from Delta Force, Task Force Orange, and other classified subunits deep behind enemy lines in such countries as Lebanon, Syria, and Iran to gather intelligence for future actions or to strike militants on the ground with missiles.

These orders were not carte blanche, because the president and secretary of state needed to sign off on dicey missions, but they increased SOF latitude substantially. The document did delineate the type of missions permitted, along with restrictions. Wide latitude existed in Afghanistan and Iraq against al Qaeda, as was to be expected, because each theater was caught up in an insurgency involving the United States and its allies. In other states, JSOC needed additional approvals from Washington officials, including the president and secretary of defense, before preparing for lethal operations. Raids into Pakistan carried stringent sanctions. In the Philippines, special operators trained Filipino counterinsurgent forces but could not fire their weapons unless directly endangered by insurgents. In other nations, such as Algeria, Mali, Nigeria, Somalia, and Syria, varied conditions needed to be met before JSOC operations could be mounted. The EXORD also set down rules of engagement as well as codified the kinds of munitions and surveillance to be used.

Given the Bush White House's warm endorsement of the new guidelines, other agencies, including the CIA, came on board, although the State Department worried about the ramifications of America's militarized foreign policy.[19] Those responsible for securing amicable international relations with other powers already felt uneasy about having CIA case officers operate under the diplomatic cover of U.S. embassies. Diplomats tried to keep as much distance as possible between themselves and their in-house spies. But the nature of the shadowy struggle against Islamist militants sheltering in the world's far reaches before stepping out to shoot or bomb their victims transformed yesteryear's rules. Not only intelligence operatives were to be housed in diplomatic posts but also civilian-dressed special operators, some of whom carried assault rifles while traveling from Kenya into unruly countries such as Somalia and Yemen. In this altered universe, SOF gained much more freedom of action, sometimes at the expense of diplomatic niceties and even the wishes of embassy-based CIA personnel.

In the meantime, the Agency's often-maligned clandestine service's paramilitary activities in fact served well the overall initial U.S. armed incursion against al Qaeda and its Taliban hosts. Small teams of CIA field operatives (some of whom were former SOF troopers) cemented U.S.–Northern Alliance cooperation in the earliest days of the American incursion into Afghanistan. Indeed, the Northern Alliance chiefs more readily welcomed civilian-dressed personnel than militarily uniformed Special Forces detachments. The Afghan resistance, no matter how desperate their position vis-à-vis the Taliban, proved reluctant to open its doors to camouflage-clad troops. The Red Army's occupation left an indelible mark on the country. The Northern Alliance also clashed with its would-be benefactors over what targets to bomb and which drop zones to use for reinforcements and resupply. Gary Schroen, in his firsthand account of the intervention, *First In: An Insider's Account of How the CIA Spearheaded the War on Terror in Afghanistan*, recounts the interallied feuds. The head of the Northern Alliance after the bombing assassination of Ahmad Shah Masood (its charismatic chieftain), General Mohammad Fahim Khan, requested that A-Teams wear civilian clothing when operating with Northern Alliance militia, but the Special Forces wore military uniforms.[20] The Afghan sensitivity about foreign-uniformed soldiers in their midst points to an advantage of civilian officials working inside hypernationalistic countries that might have experienced colonial occupations, such as Libya, Somalia, and Algeria.

Sweetness and light did not always prevail between warriors and spies as their joint mission unfolded. Starting two months into the Afghan incursion, isolated cases of friction began to occur. For example, CIA actions in the Ghazni area not far from the Pakistani border sparked tension with the U.S. Central Command. A CIA team's request for airlift for itself and a couple of captured low-level Taliban suspects reportedly miffed CENTCOM because it had not been informed beforehand of the Agency's activity in Ghazni. CENTCOM relented, in part, because JSOC operatives accompanied the CIA teams.[21] These and similar petty verbal feuds, I must stress, never hindered the overall offensive. Both the Northern Alliance and in-country CIA officers expressed dissatisfaction with the Pentagon and CENTCOM over air strikes, which aimed more at military infrastructure than initially at the Taliban front lines. Schroen later pointed to smooth cooperation when the remotely piloted Predators took flight in Afghan skies.[22]

The Jawbreaker leader, however, aired his frustration at a Delta Force unit's rescue plans to free staff members of a Christian humanitarian group known as Shelter Now International, who had been imprisoned by the Taliban in Kabul. He wrote, "None of them had any real idea of the situation on the ground in Afghanistan."[23] Schroen was relieved when the unit dropped its "simple plan." The CIA officer concluded that "even the three Delta operators realized the plan was both impossible and lame, and we never heard any more from [them] on the rescue plan."[24]

As events turned out, Schroen's negative judgment was greatly misplaced and incomplete. JSOC never stopped planning for a hostage rescue mission. In fact, back at Fort Bragg, it painstakingly rehearsed a rescue plan at a specially constructed mock-up of the Kabul prison. Just before the rescue team launched the recovery operation, the Taliban hostage takers fled Kabul as the city fell to the U.S.-supported Northern Alliance militias. Airlifting the eight hostages from the still-dangerous capital necessitated a daring helicopter insertion. The famed Night Stalker pilots (the nickname for JSOC's 160th Special Operations Aviation Regiment) flew a cumbersome Chinook helicopter, guarded by SEAL operators, into an improvised pickup zone. After delivering the foreign humanitarian workers to safety, the two pilots received a phone call from President Bush.[25]

The doubts about each other's competency were not a one-way street, with only the CIA holding misgivings about SOF and their bold approaches. For their part, some SOF held skeptical opinions about CIA operatives without military backgrounds until they proved themselves under fire. If the Agency men demonstrated shooting and other soldiering skills, then they won over, or at least received grudging acceptance from, the special operators. Lest we forget, it was a CIA paramilitary officer, Johnny Michael Spann from the Special Activities Division, who became the first CIA paramilitary officer killed after the U.S. intervention into Afghanistan. He was predeceased by a few days by two Army Rangers who died in an assault on an airfield.[26] Hence, SOF and CIA personnel, not conventional forces, suffered the initial casualties in the new war on terrorism.

Despite the moderate on-the-ground friction, and even the inevitable snarled communications between "men on the spot" and their continental U.S. headquarters many time zones away, the SOF-CIA liaison functioned well, aside from the inevitable Clausewitzian "frictions" of war, such as confusion and unexpected events. Disputes were more frequent between CIA field operatives and their Langley headquarters or between the Agency and CENTCOM than any SOF-CIA interactions. The "man-on-the spot" often chafes at perceived restraints from headquarters. For example, the Jawbreaker head complained to the CIA's Counterterrorism Center over coordination issues.[27] Overall, though, the "jointness" of SOF-CIA during the initial U.S. intervention phase functioned as effectively as it did in the next phase.

The respective capabilities of special military personnel and intelligence field officers complemented each other to defeat the Taliban regime. Their integration pointed toward the fusion of the warrior and intelligence communities later in Afghanistan, Iraq, and elsewhere that removed so many terrorist-insurgent chiefs from the battlefield. U.S. Army colonel Kathryn Stone, while a student at the U.S. Army War College, summed up the budding partnership in one sentence after President Bush's order to use "all means necessary" to defeat al Qaeda: "This order in turn generated an operationally-driven ad hoc relationship between CIA paramilitary operatives and SOF on the ground in Afghanistan that resulted in improved lethality and agility on the battlefield stemming from each group's distinct contribution to warfighting."[28]

During the first months of the American-led incursion, Special Operations Forces and CIA field operatives were again thrown together in the hunt for Osama bin Laden in the Tora Bora mountains bordering Pakistan. The Delta Force operators relied on the CIA representatives for intelligence about local strongmen and for abundant cash to bring over key figures for their mission. The CIA officials also acted as translators for the special operations strike teams in the mountainous terrain. In the pursuit of the terrorist mastermind, one Agency officer was also given the task of providing "firsthand reporting of attitudes, performance, and genuine effort."[29] His source was the local Afghan militia under Hazrat Ali, a warlord employed by the CIA to help SOF track down the Saudi-born terrorist. The joint team of field officers and operators never met up with their elusive quarry. Bin Laden either escaped during the earlier phrase of the allied intervention or later slipped through the porous border, which many argued should have been sealed by large numbers of U.S. ground troops. Yet little intra-team criticism resounded among the participants about the failings of spies or assaulters. Indeed, the senior-ranking SOF officer during the chase over the perilous icy cliffs to corner bin Laden lauded an Arabic-speaking CIA officer whose actions "likely saved the lives of several" SOF operators.[30]

The CIA's initial mission soon shifted from the initial go-between role to facilitate the SOF–Northern Alliance partnership to the nearly single-minded pursuit of the al Qaeda hierarchy, especially Osama bin Laden. But the Agency's CTC also trained its sights on Taliban leaders in Pakistan so as to kill them through drone attacks or even commando raids run by JSOC. Coordination took place between U.S. Navy SEALs and CIA field operatives working out of Bagram Air Base on the outskirts of Kabul in the first months after the start of the Afghan war. Their cooperation formed another nucleus for a broader synergy later, such as the Omega Program, to be discussed subsequently. Suffice it to say for now that the teamwork opened ways for the SEAL shooters to function as the Agency's hit squad, while the CIA furnished intelligence to SEAL teams for targeted raids against local Taliban functionaries in southeastern Afghanistan.[31] The special assault troops operated in the shadows as nearly invisible warriors, much as spies performed.

The drone missiles that struck militants in Pakistani territory remained in CIA hands because, nominally, Pakistan was a close ally of the United States. The unacknowledged air strikes, therefore, fell into the covert category. The CIA also turned to its own devices for paramilitary forces, a role they fulfilled during the Korean and Vietnam Wars. Its Special Activities Division employed field officers who trained, advised, and even armed indigenous forces, much as the Special Forces did under the Joint Special Operations Command.

As first revealed in his 2010 book, *Obama's Wars*, Bob Woodward described Langley's exclusive ground force in Afghanistan under the title of Counterterrorism Pursuit Teams (CTPT). Woodward wrote that the CTPT were the "CIA's 3,000-man covert army." Authorized by President George W. Bush, these teams "were a paid, trained and functioning tool of the CIA."[32] They staged multiple raids against the Taliban with ties to al Qaeda in the south around Kandahar. Woodward also reported that the CTPT conducted "cross-border operations into Pakistan."[33] Another source noted that the CIA paid Ahmed Wali Karzai, the Afghan president's half-brother, to hire gunmen for an Agency-trained militia known as the Kandahar Strike Force. Based in Kandahar, Wali Karzai was a local power broker before his assassination by a bodyguard. Marinated in corruption, Wali Karzai was considered a corrosive figure in southern Afghanistan by top U.S. generals, reportedly including David McKiernan and Stanley McChrystal.[34]

The CIA's militia organizing could have thrown another wrench in the military-spy machinery. Set up, trained, and directed by the SAD within the Agency's National Clandestine Service, the CTPT and its full range of activities remains murky but includes disrupting insurgent networks, collecting intelligence, and conducting kinetic operations against low-level and high-level Taliban figures.[35] Accomplishing its disruptive missions against the Taliban meant crossing into Pakistan. These not-so-secret teams served to police the border until the Afghan army was trained and equipped to take over the role.

One expert has commented that the CIA's shadow army was often regarded by the U.S. forces as "answerable to no one, and by and large they were not."[36] Regular U.S. military personnel, including special operations members, held that these CIA-organized auxiliaries confused local Afghans about the nature of their defenders and their connection to the central government. American officers argued that the CTPT should be folded into the regular Afghan National Army and that the CIA should return to its traditional pursuits of collecting and analyzing strategic intelligence. The "spats" that broke out on the ground, however, "flared up over personalities and prerogatives."[37] Despite coordination issues among various units, SOF and the Pentagon accepted the CIA's paramilitary operations rather than objecting to them on the grounds that standing up opposition units was usually a prerogative of the Special Forces. Harmony and cooperation were more highly prized in war zones than turf battles.

In 2013, these undercover Afghan militias titularly commanded by the Afghan security agency, the National Directorate of Security, resurfaced in the media. According to two journalists, the CIA "paramilitaries known as 0–4 Unit, a so-called Counterterrorist Pursuit Team,"[38] were involved in a supposedly botched raid in Kunar Province. The Karzai government revealed the operation as a means to criticize certain U.S. military initiatives, a recurring theme from the former Kabul regime. The Kabul government frequently scorned SOF night raids and opposed U.S. efforts to establish Afghan local police units. President Karzai regarded the new local police as akin to private armies presided over by warlords beyond his control or patronage. They stood to weaken the central government's outreach efforts to the countryside.

The seventy-five-man police units were advised by four paramilitary officers and funded by the CIA, which linked the units to the National Directorate of Security. What was less apparent in these print accounts was that the 0–4 Unit and other U.S.-trained military groups were being groomed for the eventual American and coalition drawdown of combat troops in 2014.[39] The CIA and SOF prepared local forces to take over lead roles in combating the Taliban and their allies among al Qaeda and the Haqqani network (which operated independently of the Taliban, much as a warlord movement) while they lowered their public visibility in line with Washington's evolving global counterterrorism strategy. But at least one unit of the CIA-trained CTPT went rogue, with extortion, residential raids, and killings in the eastern province of Khost as most of the U.S. ground combat units departed from Afghanistan. The Khost Protection Force, made up of 3,500 fighters and nominally subordinate to the National Directorate of Security, in reality operated autonomously from the Kabul government. Like other units of the CTPT, it refused to take orders from its political masters in the capital, which still depended on the effectiveness of the Khost Protection Force to provide security against the resurgent Taliban militants.[40] So this unit of the CTPT resembled a big city police force that arrests street thugs while wrongfully shooting whom it pleases in other confrontations.

An exposé-type article in the *New York Times* written by a team of reporters detailed the collaboration of SEAL Team 6 and the Central Intelligence Agency in a manner that "blurred the traditional lines between soldier and spy," as intelligence officers performed paramilitary duties and special shooters took up spying missions. Members from the intelligence side and the operations side joined together in an initiative called the Omega Program. Because it functioned under the CIA, the Omega Program enjoyed greater latitude with "deniable operations" to carry out missions in the shadows to hunt down and eliminate mid-to-low-level Taliban adversaries within Afghanistan. Some of the pursuit techniques wielded by the Omega Program had been pioneered by Delta Force in Iraq a few years earlier. The newspaper journalists also compared the interrogations and assassinations to the Vietnam-era Phoenix Program, which garnered much unfavorable commentary in the 1970s. The Omega Program, like its earlier Phoenix counterpart, sought to dismantle the hidden insurgent infrastructure in the Afghan country-side by going after bomb makers and local subcommanders. Between 2006 and 2008, the SEAL operators each night logged a score or more of operations that notched as many as ten to fifteen kills nightly.[41]

General McChrystal, then the JSOC commander, relied on the SEALs to retrieve the deteriorating coalition war effort in Afghanistan because Washington's attention had turned to the raging Iraq insurgency during the mid-2000s. SEAL Team 6 members participated in the covert Omega Program, along with CIA paramilitary officers and Afghan fighters who were recruited and instructed by the Agency's SAD. Together they staged raids into Pakistan, but when Islamabad objected strenuously to Washington, the Omega Program switched to attacks mainly within Afghanistan.

Like some Delta Force operators, Team 6's Black Squadron dressed in mufti and conducted "advance force operations," a military term meaning reconnaissance activities prior to SOF engagements. Like elements of Task Force Orange, Black Squadron personnel mimicked CIA spies and ventured into nations not at war with the United States in the Middle East, Africa, and Latin America to eke out information. To disguise their activities, the Black Squadron permitted women in its ranks. A male-female couple attracted less scrutiny from hostile intelligence services. This technique came to be labeled "profile softening" and enabled the military-turned-spy participants to blend into local crowds more easily than a single male. Their activities sometimes duplicated the Langley operatives, but turf battles were kept out of the public eye.[42]

In the immediate years after the intervention into Afghanistan by the military and civilian cloak-and-dagger men, the American military commanders grew to distrust the spy agency. They held the CIA in low regard for its lack of information about Taliban attacks launched from Pakistan that killed far too many U.S. troops. American officers wanted reliable information about impending attacks. General David McKiernan (who preceded General McChrystal) suspected that CIA dispatches "were spoon-fed by Pakistani spies."[43] Like his predecessors, the new commander of the International Security Assistance Force (ISAF; the overall umbrella organization for all foreign troops in Afghanistan) blamed Pakistan for not doing enough to suppress militancy in its tribal belt bordering Afghanistan. The ISAF commander was particularly irked at Pakistan for not providing warnings to NATO forces across the frontier of impending Taliban assaults. So convinced did the ISAF general become of CIA ineptitude and so rivalrous had military-CIA interaction become that he approved a $22 million contract with AfPax Insider, a private contractor, to ferret out intelligence inside Pakistan through a network of former CIA officers and onetime SOF troops. In brief, McKiernan was trying an end run around the Agency. Not unexpectedly, the CIA tried to block the deal employing a private spying operation. Eventually, the AfPax Insider scheme was closed down when the contract funds dried up in May 2010, but the episode revealed the deep reservoir of distrust and anger by some high-ranking military officials at the CIA.[44]

Overlapping with the AfPax Insider caper was an official U.S. military spy venture that also competed with Langley's intelligence endeavors. This intelligence-gathering and reconnaissance enterprise took up where Donald Rumsfeld's expansive 2003 Al Qaeda Network Executive Order left off. It was also another illustration of the military's enlarging human-spying efforts. Secretary Rumsfeld departed from the Pentagon in late 2006. Two years later, the entire Bush administration departed from

Washington. Rather than abandoning its predecessor's policies as expected, the incoming Barack Obama presidency doubled down on many. The drone campaigns represented one such endeavor. And the special operations spying and secret wars in Yemen and elsewhere constituted others.

In this vein, the Obama White House permitted its CENTCOM commander, General David Petraeus, to issue a broad directive. In late September 2009, the four-star commander set forth in the Joint Unconventional Warfare Task Force Execute Order a wide-scoped clandestine military and intelligence operation to counter threats and disrupt militant groups in the Middle East, Central Asia, and the Horn of Africa. The task force embraced the mission "to prepare the environment" for any future combat operations in both hostile nations, such as Iran, and friendly ones, such as Saudi Arabia and Jordan.[45] The order granted permission to Task Force Orange to engage in human spying along with its electronic capabilities into countries beyond the declared war zones in Iraq and Afghanistan. Newspaper accounts reported that Petraeus drafted his order in close coordination with Admiral Eric T. Olson, then in charge of Special Operations Command. The CENTCOM execute order "aggressively pushed the military deeper into the CIA's turf, using Special Operations troops and private contractors to conduct secret intelligence missions."[46] Outsiders speculated that the execute order was another military step to lessen dependency on the CIA in gaining battlefield intelligence in Pakistan and other non-war-zone countries. Yet, the Central Intelligence Agency raised no public opposition. Indeed, a CIA spokesman characterized the Pentagon and CIA as sharing a "close relationship." He praised in-field coordination that "typically works well, and if problems arise, they get settled."[47]

Threats compelled the United States to pay attention to developments in East Asia as well. Thousands of leagues away from the CENTCOM's battlespaces, George W. Bush's Pentagon retrained its sights on the Philippines, where a fresh threat arose from Islamist-inspired bandits. Before this renewed attention, the Pentagon had long enjoyed a conspicuous presence on the Pacific archipelago, dating back to the fears of Communist insurgency during the Cold War. After the Philippines attained its independence from the United States in 1946, the island nation endured a Communist-led insurgency and a violent resistance among the Muslim population in the country's southern islands. The United States stood by the Manila governments with counterinsurgency training and supplies of advanced weaponry. The Filipinos opened their territory to the Pentagon. America's Navy and Air Force resided on two large bases within the archipelagic state. The Central Intelligence Agency ran one of its largest overseas stations in the Philippines to collect intelligence and run operations throughout East Asia at the height of the Cold War.

In early 2002, Washington stepped up its assistance to the armed forces of the Philippines after an American missionary couple—Martin and Gracia Burnham—were taken hostage by Abu Sayyaf (this name came from Afghan jihadi Abdul Rasul Sayyaf and means roughly "Bearer of the Sword") the previous May. The Abu Sayyaf group carried out thuggery, kidnapping for ransom, and murder in the southernmost islands, which were largely populated by Muslims. The horrific 9/11 events propelled the obscure Abu Sayyaf group, which swore allegiance to Osama bin Laden, onto the American counterterrorism screen. The Bush administration offered Manila intelligence-backed counterterrorism assistance. Gloria Macapagal Arroyo, the Philippine president, accepted the offer with some strings attached. The Pentagon and Central Intelligence Agency answered the call and dispatched personnel to the East Asian nation.

Because of the decades of U.S. semicolonial rule, the Filipino people were acutely sensitive to preserving their independence from its giant benefactor on the other side of the Pacific. Consequently, when the Defense Department established the Joint Special Operations Task Force–Philippines, the Manila government laid down conditions when it signed the Visiting Forces Agreement with Washington. Chiefly, it prohibited the six hundred SOF and other personnel from engaging in direct combat with Islamist insurgents. To maintain a Filipino control over the military operations, the task force limited the American contingent to advising and assisting the local security forces. The SOF and the CIA role focused on manhunting rather than a full-blown insurgency.[48] Thirteen years after announcing Operation Enduring Freedom–Philippines, the Pentagon pulled some of its troops out of the country, but the Philippine campaign served as a model for Barack Obama's "hub" strategy on the other side of the globe, to be noted later in this book.

The Evolving SOF-CIA Partnership

After the intervention phase of the Afghan war ended, the close SOF-CIA relationship initially departed from its tight warrior-spy collaboration involved in marshaling the Northern Alliance's militias to toss out the Taliban regime. As the Agency came to center its attention on top al Qaeda figures, its close links to the U.S. military frayed as incoming conventional warfighters busied themselves with battling a retreating and disarrayed Taliban militia. The NATO ground forces turned to developing civil services and government functions. Distrust grew among the top military brass about the reliability of CIA intelligence pinpointing the whereabouts of bin Laden and Ayman al-Zawahiri, his deputy and an Egyptian medical doctor. In spring 2002, the spy agency's intelligence did not pan out on bin Laden's whereabouts.[49] Given the ultimate masterful raid that took down the "Pacer" (the CIA nickname for bin Laden because he often paced the confines of his Pakistani compound), it behooves students of the SOF-CIA liaison to note that their relationship was not made in heaven despite many harmonious interactions. The eventual close SOF-CIA linkage over time was brought about by the exertions of "men on the spot" in Afghanistan and Iraq in spite of the distinct mandates and identities of their respective communities.

As Agency officers joined with SOF operators to form a fusion cell at Bagram airfield to collect and analyze intelligence, the CIA field operatives also established their own outposts in eastern Afghanistan. They collected information from CIA "assets" coming across the border from the tribal areas in Pakistan. These Pakistani informants met with their spy handlers at the Afghan bases or nearby towns. Langley sent requests to the CIA bases for information on the location of militants in Pakistan's South Waziristan region. The intelligence gleaned from tipsters as well as from satellites and cell phone transmissions was compiled and analyzed for drone targeting or commando raids. Human source information was vital to the identification process.

One such base came to public attention when things went terribly wrong. Bent on bringing bin Laden to justice, Langley appointed one of its most talented and experienced officers, Jennifer Matthews, with the task of vetting a potential high-level informant at Forward Operating Base Chapman in Khost, located in eastern Afghanistan near the Pakistani border. But the CIA was not the only scorpion in the bottle. For its part, al Qaeda sought relief from frequent aerial assaults from CIA drones. The terrorist network hatched a deadly plot against its nemesis. At the CIA base, Matthews stood near the center of the Agency's authenticating process for Humam al-Balawi (a nom de guerre for Abu Dujanah al-Khorasani), a Jordanian pediatrician. Balawi was considered a reliable spy for penetration of al Qaeda by Jordan's well-regarded intelligence service for assessing violent Islamic extremism. In fact, Balawi was a double agent. After convincing U.S. and Jordanian intelligence officials of his trustworthiness, Balawi traveled through Pakistan to Khost, where Matthews eased the way for his border crossing and relaxed the defensive protocols for his entry into the CIA quarters within the Chapman forward operating base. When Matthews and her fellow officers greeted Balawi, he detonated a bomb in his coat. The blast killed Matthews and six other CIA officials and contractors on December 30, 2009.

This suicide attack was the biggest loss for the Agency since the April 8, 1983, car bombing of the U.S. Embassy in Beirut, Lebanon, which killed eight CIA workers, including the station chief. The deaths at the Chapman base steeled the CIA's determination to hunt down bin Laden and other top terrorists. It also led almost immediately to a leap in the number of drone strikes on al Qaeda, the Haqqani network, and Taliban leaders inside Pakistan. Within a year of the Khost bombing, most of Balawi's accomplices met death by drone missiles.[50] But even this fact did not slake Langley's thirst for revenge against al Qaeda and its rarely seen ringleader.

After the al Qaeda leadership fled to Pakistan in late 2001, they enjoyed sanctuary and a degree of safety. Gradually, the CIA and the Joint Special Operations Command wore away at al Qaeda's safe haven next door through commando raids and, especially, drone strikes. The U.S. security forces tracked, monitored, targeted, and neutralized several senior Taliban and al Qaeda figures. SOF laid plans for cross-border raids to kill or capture their targets, only to have most attacks canceled because of Washington's concerns about violating Pakistan's sovereignty.

A small number of operations were executed before the dramatic takedown of Osama bin Laden. American political leaders worried that sending in squads of elite warriors would undermine Pakistani president Pervez Musharraf's hold on power. Because of the ferocious anti-U.S. demonstrations in the country's streets, a high-profile U.S. incursion could destabilize Pakistan.

Administration officials dealt with JSOC requests for more reliable intelligence in 2006. They pushed Langley to dispatch more field operatives to the war zone to work alongside SOF to collect and analyze information about al Qaeda in Pakistan and nearby countries. Washington also ratcheted up its deployment of intelligence personnel and shadow warriors in Yemen, Libya, Somalia, and, later, Mali, while unveiling its evolving strategy for addressing the proliferation of al Qaeda franchises in poorly governed countries in the Middle East and Africa.[51] It also turned to the frustrations and concerns about "invading" Pakistan with a platoon or more of SOF operators. A less-intrusive means to extend the lethal reach of American power were remotely piloted aircraft. These so-called drones lurked overhead for hours, transmitting real-time video feeds back to ground controllers, where analysts monitored and studied them for potential targeting. Drones, such as the Predators and Reapers, rained down deadly missiles on their targets with pinpoint precision, which often spared the lives of close-by innocents. Begun in the waning years of the Bush administration with just a few drone air strikes aimed at terrorist fugitives sheltering in Pakistan, the drone attacks accelerated with the Obama presidency, as will be described at greater length below. Thus, the evolving triad of the CIA, SOF, and drones pointed toward the counterterrorism strategy for the near-term future. The SOF-CIA partnership came to be characterized by a light military footprint, drones for surveillance or lethal strikes, and train-and-assist missions for host-nation forces.

As this security architecture unfolded, it was calculated to make counterterrorism more streamlined, surgical, acceptable, and financially affordable to a badly cash-strapped and war-weary America.

Feuds, Fusion, and the Joint Interagency Task Force

The terrorist-based insurgencies that emerged first in Iraq, then Afghanistan, and next in Pakistan, Yemen, and finally Africa prompted a greater push for SOF-CIA cooperativeness. This evolving collaboration may not have replicated the seamlessness of the Nathan Hale soldier-to-spy transformation. But in human affairs, the SOF-CIA interaction attained as close a fraternity as was realistic between two different government agencies. The al Qaeda insurgency forged this not-always-perfect union out of necessity that grew even more imperative as jihadi terrorism became ever more diffuse, nebulous, and multifarious. Before that warrior-spy fusion, however, disenchantment with the intelligence community surfaced within the Pentagon's top civilian leadership.

The unexpected insurgency during the Iraq War prompted the Defense Secretary Donald Rumsfeld to express his frustration at the CIA and DIA. He opined that the Agency "failed to assess correctly the threat posed by the Fedayeen"—the irregular Iraqi resistance to the U.S. and allied intervention in the early weeks of the conflict. Broadening his criticism, the secretary continued: "The intelligence agencies failed to warn of the possibility" for "the attraction of foreign jihadists to the conflict in Iraq."[52] He also took issue with the intelligence community for "the failure to highlight the dangers of an insurgency."[53] Tension also arose within Iraq's urban centers between Delta Force and CIA field agents, as the two entered into the manhunting business.

Because the Iraqi insurgency took the Agency by surprise, it had just a few field officers in central Iraq, where the terrorism exploded. To top it off, there was no effective Iraqi intelligence service to draw on for information.

The Delta operatives struck out on their own to create an underground network of local informers. Unlike CIA operatives, they were accustomed to traveling within war zones. Moreover, they could easily settle in with the coalition military bases throughout the embattled areas. Delta teams purchased local cars to avoid attracting the attention that military vehicles would draw moving through narrow streets and alleys. They recruited and paid Iraqi agents, whom they referred to as Mohawks. These human sources were able to accomplish up-close reconnaissance of people and buildings that no Western infiltrator could safely undertake. The Mohawks also planted software on computers in Internet cafés, which sprung up after the ouster of Saddam Hussein; the dictator had kept a tight rein on access to foreign contacts. This spyware identified users and let their communications be read by SOF and the NSA. Later, the NSA built an instrument, Polarbreeze, for wirelessly tapping into close-by computers. The National Security Agency assisted JSOC elements working on the ground in Iraq to infiltrate "al-Qaeda's network of websites and servers, which Americans called Obelisk."[54] The Obelisk system functioned as al Qaeda's corporate intranet, through which the terrorist headquarters communicated with its cells, released propaganda videos, detailed financial information, and issued marching orders to fighters. Once the soldier-spies penetrated this command-and-control structure, the NSA hackers relayed tactical bulletins to Delta units, which engaged the fighters, funders, or enablers. They also embedded spyware and malicious software to access intelligence and to disrupt the circuitry of the terrorist group.[55]

In late 2004, the National Security Agency fielded a secret device that Delta operators called "the find" because it enabled them to locate a cell phone and its owner even when the phone was turned off. Their adversaries' phones turned out to be tracking gadgets. The signals emitted from the enemies' cell phones were plotted on maps, allowing Delta members to capture, kill, or call in an air strike on their elusive foes. Years afterward, one specialized unit estimated that it located thousands of insurgents, including scores of al Qaeda in Iraq, by this technique. When this electronic locater was used to pinpoint the facilitators or financiers of terrorism, it proved particularly disruptive to the terror network in western Iraq.[56]

As the Delta personnel developed their own human sources, they incurred resentment from CIA officials, who by 2004 were establishing themselves on military bases within greater Baghdad.[57] In another operational field, the Agency proved reluctant to concur with a JSOC mission to penetrate Iran with a clandestine team. The purpose was to ascertain whether an undercover two-person team from Task Force Orange could get close to suspected Iranian nuclear sites. The Central Intelligence Agency considered such deep-cover operations as falling under its purview. After the CIA grudgingly agreed, the mission went forward in late 2004. Orange concluded that it was possible to get close enough to the nuclear installations to take telltale soil samples. But the Orange twosome did not take the samples; they just established the feasibility of doing so. The turf struggles, nonetheless, exacerbated SOF-CIA animosities.[58]

To ease the growing tensions with the Agency, McChrystal dispatched his talented intelligence chief, then colonel Michael Flynn (years later as a four-star general he headed the Defense Intelligence Agency), to serve as his liaison to the CIA station in Baghdad on its way to becoming the largest such apparatus in the world. When the Agency's CTC personnel were brought into JSOC fusion cells along with SOF, FBI, and others, the animosity eased. But these early recriminations and frictions highlight how dramatic the later SOF-CIA fusion became, given the disharmony swirling through the early stages of the conflict against insurgent-based terrorism in Iraq.

Despite the secretary of defense's strongly held views about the Agency, his Special Operations Forces depended on CIA field officers in Iraq's Kurdistan region before the U.S. ground invasion of Iraq. During the summer of 2002, Agency teams in Kurdistan and nearby countries introduced special operations troops to Iraqi commanders and others, who convinced some in Saddam Hussein's officer corps to surrender rather than fight. The intelligence professionals also furnished tactical information useful for U.S paratrooper drops in the country's northern reaches as part of the larger intervention.[59]

The Iraq War started as an air-land blitzkrieg offensive toward Baghdad. The United States, along with Britain, which fielded the second-largest ground force, engaged Iraq's Republican Guard in late March 2003. America's highly rapid and explosive "shock and awe" phase demolished Saddam Hussein's tank-and-infantry-style army within three weeks. This high-intensity combat gave way to an anti-Western insurgency and sectarian conflict between Sunni and Shiite residents. Insurgency and terrorism demanded approaches far different from regular military operations. To combat shadowy insurgents and stealthy bomb-laying terrorists, the counterinsurgent requires intelligence to find and strike the enemy while trying to predict and protect against the next assault. At the time, it was fashionable to speak about the need for a network to defeat a network. A counter-network needs to operate on the basis of the F3EAD acronym, meaning Find, Fix, Finish, Exploit, Analyze, and Disseminate. Finding terrorists, fixing their location, and finishing them off proved an inadequate response without exploiting intelligence seized during operations and then analyzing as well as disseminating it for future missions. The integration of these elements required the blurring of the lines between intelligence gathering and soldiering, a process driven by a new JSOC general officer.

The Joint Special Operations Command (known for security reasons as Task Force 714) underwent a transformation when then major general Stanley McChrystal took command in October 2003. The general built on the lessons gained from the SOF and CIA cooperation on manhunts in Colombia and Bosnia. McChrystal realized that JSOC (or TF 714) had to leverage intelligence assets to hunt down terrorists in Iraq, where al Qaeda and other like-minded jihadi networks were intensifying their bombings and shootings. As noted earlier, the two-star officer set up the JIATF, which in time incorporated the CIA and other intelligence departments. He also brought to the table representatives from the National Security Agency; the National Geospatial-Intelligence Agency, which conducts visual surveillance; the U.S. Central Command; and regional experts from the State Department. In the words of one author, General McChrystal reached out to entities "making deals and exchanging services, while at the same time remaining sensitive to each fiefdom's turf."[60] He placed these experts alongside JSOC personnel in the same room without partitions separating them. His goal was to break down the "stovepipes" that channeled information up and down one specialized community without sharing it with others.

To fashion and broaden his network, the impatient general dispatched more than 150 savvy JSOC liaisons to key players in the Pentagon and in the Obama government. These JSOC officers, for example, went to General Richard Myers, the chairman of the Joint Chief of Staff, General John Abizaid, CENTCOM commander, CIA director George Tenet, and the U.S. ambassadors in Pakistan and Afghanistan.[61] Their presence and participation furthered the necessary integration of warrior and intelligence communities. They also ironed out the inevitable wrinkles that flare up among government departments.

Soon after taking command, General McChrystal was caught up in the widening search for the whereabouts of Saddam Hussein. That manhunt and the worsening insurgency clarified his thinking about the nature of the struggle. Having spent much of his Army career in the direct-action Rangers, the general made the leap (in part due to the recommendation of then rear admiral William McRaven, one of TF 714's assistant commanders) in conception about how to fight al Qaeda in Iraq (AQI). McChrystal later wrote: "In addition to rewiring our own force, we must make our relationship with the intelligence agencies, particularly the CIA, deeper and broader."[62] He added that his goal was to form a true joint interagency task force. "While the concept of a JIATF was not new, it would prove a transformative step for TF 714," as he later described in his memoir.[63]

Other sources confirmed and elaborated on the course presented in the general's account. More than one commentator has noted that the "natural tendency of the intelligence community is to hoard information," but McChrystal "made his teams share intelligence."[64] JSOC built an internet that everyone in the command could access. JSOC also teamed with an intelligence unit in Fairfax, Virginia, the National Media Exploitation Center, which generated composite intelligence from torrents of information picked up from operators in the field; material included flash drives, CDs, papers, seized computers, and what was characterized as "pocket litter," scraps of paper with scrawled notes or phone numbers. The center received data from JIATF and linked it with other intelligence to produce a clearer picture of insurgent networks. Sometimes regular troops and SOF trigger pullers returned to bases from military operations with notebooks and desktops. They turned over their haul to intelligence analysts, who fed it into their "databases and used data-mining software to look for connections to other fighters either in custody or at large."[65]

General McChrystal also moved to bridge any lingering splits between the CIA and JSOC. The spies and warriors worked well within small teams in the early days of the Afghan intervention. Later, there and in Iraq, the CIA paramilitaries and civilian analysts had to depend on JSOC for safety and transport to move around the violent war theaters. This dependency "created an intense fissure between the two organizations."[66] Breaking down compartmentalization among military and intelligence units lessened the old gaps that McChrystal observed firsthand while serving on the Joint Staff preceding his JSOC command. His wartime objective aimed at an enhanced kinetic capability through a cornucopia of timely information.[67]

General McChrystal's vision went beyond only linking up with the CIA for its "human intelligence." The 24/7 access to intelligence specialists and their spies and sources was designed to improve SOF's understanding of the enemy, including its whereabouts and tactical intentions. Other intelligence agencies possessed different specialties that needed to be brought under one roof. He singled out "the National Security Agency's intercepted signals; the FBI's forensic and investigative expertise; the Defense Intelligence Agency's military reach; and the National Geospatial-Intelligence Agency's (NGA) dazzling mapping ability."[68] The DIA, for instance, had, after 9/11, greatly ramped up its "intel support" to soldiers on the ground through a difficult process likened to "building the airplane as we were flying it."[69] The DIA established the Strategic Support Branch, whose small teams were schooled in counterinsurgency and counterterrorism. They interrogated, analyzed, and even ran agents to pass tactical information in real time to frontline commanders.[70]

While the DIA expanded its ranks, SOCOM added a reported seven hundred intelligence specialists to SOF teams planning and preparing missions in Tampa and in regional theater commands to supply actionable military intelligence.[71] Another mission of this amplified martial intelligence capability hit a nerve with the CIA. Secretary Rumsfeld had ordered that some of the specialists be deployed to countries not yet active threats or still low-priority targets in the U.S. war on terrorism. Among them were Indonesia, Somalia, Yemen, and the Republic of Georgia. Their missions included scouting geographical terrain to assist future SOF assignments and conducting military-type reconnaissance of targets. Because the United States was not at war with the designated states, the CIA raised questions in what was seen as a turf war between the warriors and spies. The Agency interpreted Rumsfeld's ambitions as an infringement on its traditional role. The Pentagon countered that it was not recruiting agents in these countries—a hallowed CIA practice—and that its undercover military specialists worried about a different set of priorities.[72]

Besides the DIA, the ultra-secret Intelligence Support Activity, in part, concentrated on fine-grained battle assessments, such as a target's architecture, approaches, and armaments. The ISA specialized in on-the-ground military intelligence, using electronic eavesdropping and human-collection methods.[73] One of its devices allowed it to track cell phones that drone missiles could home in on for a kill. As noted above, the Activity's missteps during the early 1980s nearly finished it off. By September 11th, it had undergone the name change to Gray Fox and then to Task Force Orange and played a part in SOF-CIA covert operations in Somalia and nearby Ethiopia in 2006. Phoenix-like, ISA arose from bureaucratic ashes to serve as Rumsfeld's cornerstone for the Pentagon's own intelligence wing. The defense secretary upped its budget and linked it more closely with JSOC.[74]

The *9/11 Commission Report* provided a strong justification for the Pentagon because it recommended that "the lead responsibility for directing and executing paramilitary operations, whether clandestine or covert, should shift to the Defense Department" from the CIA.[75] The commission excoriated the intelligence agency for its failure to kill Osama bin Laden during the Clinton administration, when the arch-terrorist roamed visibly in Afghanistan. The panel likewise concluded that the Agency's clandestine operations suffered from severe dysfunction. The recommendations pointed toward a necessary reorientation of the CIA akin to its founding 1947 remit of concentrating on intelligence gathering and analysis. In that role, the Agency acted to inform the nation's policy makers, especially about the Soviet Union's military and nuclear advances. A few years after the commission's report, President George W. Bush requested a study that came out against the 9/11 Commission's recommendation, arguing that the CIA should keep its paramilitary capacity.[76] The tit-for-tat exchanges reflected little other than another round in the long-running bout between the Agency's paramilitary programs and the Defense Department's undercover operations. For some, the lines between the two government agencies shone brighter and clearer than ever. A blurring appeared impossible.

In the dueling Pentagon-Agency interactions, the Defense Department saw a way to expand its reach "if it could make the case that the United States was at war inside a country—or might be at some point in the future" without relying on the CIA.[77] Rumsfeld and his closest aides promoted the expanded use of SOF based, in part, on a loophole in the 1991 Intelligence Authorization Act. This statute mandated that the White House notify

House and Senate intelligence committees when it issued a finding—official instructions—to the CIA to engage in a covert action.[78] This finding authorized and explained the need for the secret operation. But the Department of Defense was exempt from the requirement if it asserted that its secret actions were considered traditional military activities. Coupled with the landmark Authorization for the Use of Military Force that was passed in the wake of the September 11th attacks, the Intelligence Authorization Act opened a crack for the Pentagon. The Authorization for the Use of Military Force, after all, spelled out that the United States was at war not with a particular country but with a terrorist network. This antiterrorist conflict took America into any country where al Qaeda operated. These legislative acts, then, provided the license craved by Rumsfeld to conduct a global war on terror.[79] Over time, the Pentagon and its weapon of choice, the Special Operations Forces, rushed to a globalized antiterror mission.

The way the Rumsfeld inner circle saw things, if the CIA could undertake paramilitary operations, then the Pentagon could manage its own intelligence business. The defense secretary's frustration with Langley was stated in his memoir, *Known and Unknown*.[80] Besides, Pentagon intelligence officials pulled together detailed images of targets that commanders prized to achieve lopsided victories without U.S. casualties.[81] Concerns about muscling in on each other's territory made the eventual close cooperation between SOF and the CIA all the more remarkable as America girded for a long war on terrorists.

Before the SOF-CIA convergence, Rumsfeld expressed reservations about the reliability of CIA intelligence, especially in light of the spy agency's failure regarding Iraq's phantom nuclear and chemical weapons stockpiles, which proved nonexistent. In 2005, for example, he scrubbed the special operators' participation in a CIA-reconnoitered cross-border raid into Bajaur, Pakistan. In Washington, the two security organizations locked horns over which entity should take the lead in combating global terrorism. In their competition, they were taking over each other's functions. The Pentagon stepped up its intelligence collection and evaluation. The CIA's paramilitary branch was in the ascendency with its accelerating killer-drone campaign. Gradually, changes in leadership brought about improved relations. The aborted Bajaur attack even contributed to paving the way for greater cooperation between special operators and case officers. When another opportunity arose for a SEAL-CIA strike into Pakistan in 2006, it won approval and proceeded against the village of Damadola. Although the operation netted no key al Qaeda figures, it did signal the cementing of cooperative procedures. In the sprawling Pakistani port of Karachi, a clandestine American team of Agency case officers and SOF troops worked together to uncover Afghan Taliban networks.[82] The cooperative operations in the field spoke clearer than words in Washington.

chapter six

The SOF–CIA Fusion Concept
in Two Theaters

IN IRAQ, General McChrystal's fusion concept moved beyond previous attempts with interagency task forces before the 9/11 suicide hijackers. These clearinghouse activities within the Unites States often failed because, in his words, "the Beltway culture compelled, or allowed, the agencies to be less collaborative."[1] Such Washingtonian factors as bureaucratic inertia, which slowed the timely transference of information to hands needing it to act quickly in high-risk operations, stood in the way of interagency cooperation. So McChrystal pulled together the JIATF analysis of intelligence downrange, close to the fight under "the same literal tent."[2] The former Ranger commander succeeded in fashioning a hybrid military and intelligence unit that drew together soldiers and spies.

Because the anti-American insurgency first skyrocketed in Iraq, the U.S. Army general initially focused his main attention on the tidal waves of insurgent killings in the Persian Gulf country. In 2005, McChrystal moved JIATF-West from Camp Nama (built by Saddam Hussein as a detention center) in Baghdad to Balad Air Base some fifty miles north of the Iraqi capital. He wanted a secluded location to create a team atmosphere to facilitate open information sharing among the task force participants. Each of the members was used to deeply compartmented intelligence assignments, which conditioned them to withhold information from others. McChrystal strove to eliminate the stove-piping of information at his new Balad intelligence hub. A counterpart, JIATF-East, was set up at Bagram Air Base in Afghanistan. Thus, each military theater had its own intelligence nerve center.

The hard-driving Army general set his goal for "a faster process" facilitating the fusing of timely intelligence with SOF attacks or drone air strikes. Such an outcome, he figured, lessened the "gravitational pull" of the respective intelligence headquarters. In his mind, the cooperation deepened through the sense of a "shared mission and purpose" by all the JIATF participants.[3] A fusing of disparate units was the secondary objective to the main one—taking down terrorist and insurgent cadres. But the primary mission could not succeed without the secondary goal secured.

The general officer's vision took shape amid the stark realities of quite different professional cultures among U.S. security communities, which sometimes shared a goal but often crossed swords over the actual steps in its fulfillment. In his autobiography, McChrystal wrote frankly of his difficulties with the intelligence world, especially the CIA, which formed the main intelligence partner for SOF in its hunt for terrorists. He noted that, at the start of JIATF, "special operations and the CIA worked together only marginally better than they had during Operation Eagle Claw"[4]—the doomed hostage-rescue misadventure to Tehran in 1980 that, as mentioned earlier, left bitter interagency memories. Surveying his four and one-half years on the job, he acknowledged: "I knew my Agency partners had equally mixed sentiments about me, and I admired them for their tolerance." He recounted his uneven relationship: "No alliance could be as infuriating or as productive as my relationship with the CIA."[5] He also enumerated problems the JIATF faced in its start-up, which are summarized as follows:

- Concern by the CIA that the JIATF was "liable to muck up their careful spy work."
- Worries that the JIATF would have intelligence leaks.
- Anxiety that agencies were sending employees of varied quality, some with restrictive instructions on how much assistance to provide the enlarging TF 714.
- Apprehension by government agencies about TF 714's "expanding presence in their community."[6]

The key to building the JIATF depended on volunteer associations from the CIA, FBI, DIA, and Treasury because no mandate existed for TF 714 to build a network or secure participation by other departments engaged in counterterrorism. It was largely the brainchild of McChrystal and his inner circle. As such, it did incur pushback from others because of McChrystal's straying outside a task force's traditional role. Fortunately, the evolution of TF 714 enjoyed the backing of the Pentagon and General John Abizaid, the commander of the U. S. Central Command.

To get the JIATF concept off the ground, its commander had to overcome the reluctance of other agencies to participate in building a counter network to tackle the metastasizing terrorist network clawed into existence by Abu Musab al-Zarqawi (tagged "AMZ" by U.S. troops) in central Iraq. His prominence skyrocketed to such a level that Osama bin Laden characterized Iraq as the "central front against Zionists and Crusaders."[7] Zarqawi, the pathological mastermind of AQI, unleashed a diabolical wave of terrorism against the Shia population that killed thousands of

Sunnis as well. The Jordanian terrorist sought to spark a Shiite-Sunni ethnic conflagration in his brutal offensive to establish a Sunni caliphate in Iraq and the region beyond. The near-indiscriminate nature of Zarqawi's bombing attacks in crowded squares and streets triggered a plague of violence in Baghdad and other urban centers. The wanton killing of civilians became AQI's hallmark. Other extremist movements also adopted the tactic, along with gruesome beheadings and head drillings with electrical tools that smacked of medieval tortures. Countering the elusive Zarqawi necessitated a multiagency approach to pull together all the threads from information, clues, and hunches to get a fix on the arch-terrorist. According to McChrystal, the only way to make the JIATF concept attractive to other agencies rested with being "more effective at targeting Al Qaeda for other agencies to want to join our project."[8]

Confronting Iraq's raging terrorist inferno required a course of action weighted toward timely intelligence. A significant aspect of a new strategy entailed establishing General McChrystal's TF 714 on Balad Air Base. This headquarters functioned with ultra-Spartan living conditions conducive to sharing information and focusing relentlessly on the mission to disrupt the Zarqawi network. As described by McChrystal, this facility was designed to strip away compartmentalization between military and nonmilitary personnel. But civilian departments only slowly joined the Balad network; just the CIA initially took part in the start-up phase, which occurred during the summer of 2004. By December, the FBI, NSA, National Geospatial-Intelligence Agency, and DIA had dispatched representatives to the JIATF-West base. The task force was dedicated to tracking down the al Qaeda command, bringing Zarqawi to justice, and dismantling AQI. It worked across agency lines to remove Zarqawi as the key to disemboweling his terrorist ring.[9] Before eliminating the Iraqi militant leader, JIATF-West aired videos that intended to humiliate and marginalize him by showing him fumbling an automatic rifle and ignoring a call to prayer.[10]

This lethal mission was accomplished in the early evening of June 7, 2006. Fed targeting information by the Delta Force, two F-16s bombed Zarqawi in a roadhouse surrounded by palm trees near the small town of Hibhib, northeast of Baqubah. Delta Force operators played the lead role in the lengthy monitoring of Zarqawi's contacts. Just as a courier's trail helped lead to Osama bin Laden's compound in Abbottabad, Pakistan, the path to Zarqawi's whereabouts came from surveillance of Sheik Abd al-Rahman. The sheik was a Sunni religious figure who met every seven to ten days with Iraq's chief terrorist. Not only did the air strike kill both Zarqawi and Abd al-Rahman but it also triggered a coordinated plan to take down fourteen other safe houses in Baghdad suspected of being al Qaeda nests because of the sheik's suspicious activity. Task Force 16, one of the action arms of the JIATF, also struck at other targets around the country "within twenty-four hours, before Zarqawi's network heard about the strike and scattered."[11] Months of intelligence, interrogations, and surveillance paid off in the removal of Zarqawi and chunks of his network, a deep-cutting wound but not in itself a fatal blow to AQI. Remnants lived on until the United States pulled out its last ground combat units in December 2011. Thereafter, AQI reconstituted itself as the Islamic State of Iraq and Syria (ISIS) as it joined the anti-Bashar al-Assad insurgency that engulfed Syria starting in 2011.

Task Force 714's counterterrorism mission continued to net fighters and their cadre. The number of raids, most at night, went from eighteen a month in August 2004 to ten a night, or some three hundred a month, two years later. The task force interrogators extracted tactical-level intelligence from detainees, which they immediately relayed to the SOF trigger pullers in their unit. These strike teams acted on raw intelligence gathered from raids without the requirement to wait for higher-ranking authorization in the chain of command. Operations were often based on information gathered earlier in the same day. The co-location of intelligence staffs and SOF manhunters facilitated the tight coordination and rapid response.[12] The SOF operators killed or nabbed midlevel Taliban and al Qaeda leaders along with troves of intelligence information. The task force benefited from the smooth integration of strike teams from the SEALs, Rangers, and Greens (a code name for Delta Force), lending a unity of purpose to its direct-action missions. It was also aided immeasurably by the Awakening movement among Sunni sheiks, who increasingly perceived al Qaeda as a threat to their safety and an enemy to their way of life (which included lucrative smuggling enterprises). AQI's uncompromising enforcement of the Sharia (strict religious rules of behavior) prompted the backlash.

The sheiks and their clan members reasoned that the terrorist front posed more danger to them than did the U.S. presence. Starting in the al Qaim district of northeastern Iraq during the spring of 2005, the inhabitants turned to coalition forces for assistance against their common enemy. Soon the phenomenon spread, as traditional Iraqi leaders fought back against AQI's terrorism and puritanical religious decrees. To then colonel H. R. McMaster (now a general officer) in Tal Afar or then colonel Sean MacFarland in Ramadi, both exemplars of the new counterinsurgency methodology, the disaffected Sunni leaders became quasi-allies of the United States.[13] The Marines in Fallujah experienced a similar manifestation of Sunni chieftains turning to them for help and security against AQI.[14] The task force's intelligence was also passed to U.S. Marine and Army units, which used it to pacify swaths of central Iraq.

The close coordination of conventional and special actions led, in McChrystal's words, to "a case study in the application of surgical strikes [by SOF] in support of the first two stages of what became known as the 'clear-hold-build' process of counterinsurgency."[15] The key to undercutting the Sunni extremist insurgency lay in decapitating its leadership. By relentlessly targeting the top ranks of AQI and the Kurdish group Ansar al-Sunnah, which shared an uneasy alliance, Task Force 714 and its action arm TF 16 decimated their leadership in the months following Zarqawi's death. McChrystal noted the role of intelligence in the gains while preserving the anonymity of the intelligence personnel.[16] By November 2006, his unit had stripped away Ansar al-Sunnah's topmost leadership, including local emirs, stretching from Tikrit to Baqubah and to al Qaim.

Al Qaeda in Iraq, Ansar al-Sunnah, and other Sunni extremist groups constituted just one sector of Iraq's violent networks. The Shiite population also produced terrorist groups that killed coalition soldiers. The Shiite-dominated government sitting in Baghdad relied on quasi-official police death squads to hunt down Sunni innocents as well as militants. Some Shiite militias developed from political movements that spawned their own fierce fighters who promoted their leaders' fortunes and ethnically cleansed Baghdad neighborhoods of Sunni residents. A particularly sinister organization was the "Special Groups," which Iran trained and armed. They targeted American and other coalition armored vehicles with deadly explosively formed penetrators that pierced the thickest steel plating. Carefully engineered, the explosively formed penetrators were manufactured in Iran and shipped across the border to kill Americans. To confront the Shia target sets, McChrystal fashioned a separate unit, Task Force 17, rather than dilute the focus of TF 16. The new unit and its attention on the Shia raised fresh intelligence demands. Raids on Shiite extremists sometimes involved "intelligence partners," as McChrystal referred to Iraqi civilian allies in his intelligence network.[17]

The evolving SOF-CIA mutual dependence came partially into view with Delta Force's "wet" operation against a facilitator in the AQI network. The Green operators carried out the killing, and the CIA contributed intelligence about the target and the cover of official deniability under Title 50 of the U.S. Code for covert missions. In some ways, the targeted attack served as a dress rehearsal for the killing of Osama bin Laden three years later. At the height of the Iraqi insurgency, the Green assaulters crossed into Syria, which was a noncombatant at the time. Once the operators entered into Syria, their mission went forward under the CIA mantel because the raiders clandestinely breached the sovereignty of a nation not at war with the United States.[18] The Syrian regime was complicit in the smuggling of manpower and resources to the terrorist-insurgent network through its territory into Iraq.

American forces followed the same script almost two months earlier in a ground raid into Pakistan and, much more visibly, in bin Laden's elimination. Their Syrian target was an Iraqi known by his nom de guerre Abu Ghadiya, who ran guns, money, and foreign fighters across the border into Iraq. Conducted atypically in broad daylight, the helicopter-borne Delta assault force laid siege to Abu Ghadiya's residence with a fusillade of gunfire that killed the notorious smuggler and several of his henchmen in a gun battle in late October 2008.

The Bush administration handled the Pakistani and Syrian attacks differently. The Pakistani press reaction motivated the president's National Security Council to refrain from future land-based raids into Pakistan.[19] The official backlash was a factor later in planning the killing of bin Laden by the Obama administration. Washington officials worried about Islamabad's response to the SEAL kill team's intervention.[20] After the Syrian operation, Bush officials made a spirited defense of the militant's death in order to halt the flow of material support bound for the AQI insurgency.[21] Both cross-border strikes fell under temporary CIA authority because the intended targets were in countries where Washington could not officially acknowledge combat actions.

Combining in Afghanistan

As the Iraqi conflict turned a corner by summer 2007, the Afghan insurgency picked up in intensity when the Taliban cadres reentrenched themselves in the mountainous country's southern and eastern sectors, including Kandahar, the spiritual home of the religiously motivated insurgents. The Taliban cadres regenerated themselves from bases in next-door Pakistan. Returning to Afghanistan, they adopted quasi-Maoist techniques by killing government officials and traditional village leaders and replacing them with Taliban cadre and *shuras*, or councils, to rule over the countryside. These shadow governments in the villages functioned parallel to and competed with Kabul's emasculated and often-corrupt authority. They collected "taxes" and set up tribal courts, which settled disputes and administered a rough justice. Their resurgence became noticeable to the Hamid Karzai government seated in Kabul and to its foreign allies by at least mid-2005. The fusion among JSOC and various intelligence agencies forged in Iraq ended up being exported to Afghanistan. The soldier-spy alliance changed the way the United States fought terrorism there too.

The Afghan branch of TF 714 limited its targeting to al Qaeda leaders in the Afghanistan-Pakistan border region until 2006. In that year, McChrystal turned its focus to the pursuit of the Taliban after consultation with the ISAF. William McRaven, then vice admiral, assumed command of TF 714, whose intelligence-driven campaign undercut AQI and Ansar al-Sunnah. Promoted to lieutenant general, McChrystal was assigned to the Pentagon as director of the Joint Staff (essentially he served as chief of staff to the chairman of the Joint Chiefs of Staff, Admiral Mike Mullen). Even as the Pentagon refocused its attention on the deteriorating Afghan war, American policy toward the Central Asian country underwent an overhaul following the election of Barack Obama to the White House in November 2008.

Early in 2009, following his inauguration, the new president ordered a review of the U.S. policies toward Afghanistan and Pakistan. He named Bruce Riedel, a retired career CIA analyst, to chair the White House reassessment. So even though the role was peripheral, a former CIA official played a part, together with other agencies and individuals, in developing U.S. counterinsurgency in what was becoming America's longest war. Riedel checked with the key military and civilian agencies engaged in the Afghan war. The review was "vetted through the interagency process at all levels,"[22] meaning intelligence as well as security departments. In a press briefing two months into the fledgling administration, Riedel outlined "the new strategy for Afghanistan and Pakistan."[23] Conspicuously thin on details, the "new strategy" called for what amounted to classic counterinsurgency against the Taliban. This approach meant reaching out to the Afghan population by providing security against Taliban attacks and by furnishing some essential civic services (such as clean water, electricity, medical care, and basic education) in order to win villagers over to the side of the Kabul government.

In time, implementing counterinsurgency and counterterrorism operations brought tighter SOF-CIA cooperation. Friction might have existed among personalities over mostly minor issues between the two agencies, but no major divisions hampered counterinsurgency operations. For Afghanistan, the "new strategy" simply reemphasized, in part, counterterrorist operations to "disrupt, dismantle and defeat al Qaeda." This renewed counterterrorism attention called for "increasing our intelligence focus in this theater," according to its government officials.[24]

The interaction between the special fighters and intelligence personnel surfaced publicly in two dramatic events that the media gave extensive coverage to—one a failure (the attack on the CIA outpost at Khost, as recounted earlier) and the other a victory—the death of Osama bin Laden. Before those two distinct incidents, the TF 714 footprint enlarged within Afghanistan. As the security environment worsened in Afghanistan, the Iraqi theater stabilized, allowing for the transference of resources to the Afghan theater. With that redirection came the SOF-CIA buildup in the Central Asian country. From his new ISAF commander's perch, General McChrystal requested in mid-2009 the shift of "intelligence capacity and as many strike teams as possible" from Iraq's TF 714 to its Afghan counterpart by early 2010. Admiral McRaven, according to the ISAF chief, repositioned TF 714 forces in "bases spread over most of Afghanistan." In addition, McChrystal wrote that McRaven and "his primary command team moved to Bagram," a homecoming of sorts.[25]

The SOF-CIA model of intelligence-driven assaults on terrorist-minded insurgents honed in Iraq was adapted with effective payoff in the Afghan countryside. Yet in McChrystal's mind the two theaters differed. In his book, he recounts how he took stock while riding at night in a helicopter in 2010. After persistent U.S. counterattacks in Iraq, the general penned: "We could both see and feel the impact we were having on Zarqawi's organization." In Afghanistan, on the other hand, he recorded that fighting "yielded no such mental analgesic." In fact, he concluded that "progress couldn't be measured by direct attrition of a terrorist network."[26] If anything, the Taliban insurgents were even more elusive than their Iraqi counterparts, and they enjoyed a porous border and welcoming sanctuary in Pakistan. His musing preceded the raid that netted bin Laden, however. U.S. ground force activities inside Pakistan were rare and limited to a few commando-type raids. Pakistan, as an ostensible ally and sovereign nation, escaped overt American military intervention, except for the prevalent drone flights that regularly breached its sovereignty. The CIA did station a growing number of agent-handling officers in Pakistan from mid-2006. They recruited local informants, who provided intelligence about Taliban leaders hiding out in the tribal belt along the Afghan-Pakistan border.[27] The quick processing of information enabled the Agency to target the Taliban with drone missile strikes.[28]

Killing Taliban leaders and its foot soldiers in Pakistan aided the American-led counterinsurgency effort in Afghanistan. JSOC and the CIA tracked Abu Faraj al-Libi, who was al Qaeda's number three, until arrested by Pakistani security forces in 2005. A year before his apprehension, JSOC and the CIA hatched a plan to drop a thirty-man SEAL unit into Pakistan to capture Libi (a nom de guerre of a Libyan jihadi) and possibly Ayman al-Zawahiri in a compound within the Pakistan border area. Worried about withdrawing the U.S. Navy commandos if confronted by heavier firepower, the Pentagon beefed up the raiding party by 150 Army Rangers. As noted above, Secretary Rumsfeld canceled the operation, however, out of concern that it approximated an invasion-sized force, whose presence would wash back politically on President Musharraf because of the deep anti-American sentiment in Pakistan.[29] Besides, a much more crucial raid on Pakistani soil lay in the not-too-distant future.

"Geronimo EKIA"

Osama bin Laden's death at the hands of Navy SEALS represented the end of an arduous chapter but hardly the close of the book on the widening global conflict with violent Islamist extremists. Despite the veil of secrecy that official Washington dropped to obscure the details surrounding the famous manhunt and death of al Qaeda's mastermind, many classified aspects were leaked by the administration to the news media, authors, and even the makers of the film *Zero Dark Thirty*. These accounts covered the protracted pursuit over an often-cold trail and finally the bullet-blazing elimination of the scion of a wealthy Saudi family. Bin Laden captured attention for more than a decade as a terrorist commissar who took up the sword against his homeland and much of the world to return society to a golden age of medieval Islam. His death proved even more riveting, the contours of which are well known. This summarized account, therefore, will stick with the theme of this narrative—the intertwining of special warfare operators and CIA officers.

The Central Intelligence Agency played *the* key role in the tracking and uncovering of the master terrorist's safe house in Pakistan. Moreover, U.S. clandestine activities in Pakistan largely fell under the Agency's domain. It hired former SOF personnel to perform "humint collection," or human intelligence gathered by field operatives (usually with nontechnical methods) using local tipsters for information. This does not mean that the needle-in-the-haystack search did not preoccupy SOF minds; it did. From the enlisted ranks to the multistarred commanders, bin Laden's whereabouts fixed their attention. For instance, General McChrystal even temporarily relocated his headquarters in 2007 to Afghanistan and conducted an operation—Valiant Pursuit—to "clear known or likely insurgent pockets" in the Tora Bora mountains when intelligence indicated the al Qaeda fugitive's possible presence.[30] And the petty officer in the Navy SEALs who wrote *No Easy Day* related his team's long concentration on bin Laden. He wrote of the SEAL team's frustrating return to Tora Bora in a vain search for the al Qaeda master terrorist in 2007: "We essentially bombed some empty mountains and my teammates went on a weeklong camping trip. There was no sign of any man in flowing white robes."[31]

To the SOF in pursuit of bin Laden, the Tora Bora revisit struck them as a CIA-induced wild goose chase, which led to skepticism about the Agency's intelligence work. At least one SEAL also acknowledged reciprocal sour sentiments directed by CIA personnel toward SOF operators. He wrote: "There were a lot of haters not only from the big military side but also from agency."[32] Yet, despite the occasional dyspeptic personal chemistry among particular SOF and CIA personnel, the two communities in the field locked arms in the bin Laden raid and similar in-and-out military strikes against other jihadi leaders.

Four months before the bin Laden operation, CIA director Leon Panetta invited the new JSOC commander, Vice Admiral William McRaven, to the Langley headquarters to begin preparations for a possible commando strike to capture or kill the archterrorist sheltering in Pakistan. As one writer recorded, the fact that the meeting took place at all "was a sign of how much changed in the years since 9/11" regarding SOF-CIA coordination.[33] In fact, during the run-up to the raid to take out Geronimo (the code name for Osama bin Laden by some accounts), McRaven reportedly offered immediately to "put a very seasoned member of a special unit to work directly with you [CIA officials]" on learning of the intelligence breakthrough.[34] He seconded a SEAL captain and several other planners to think through the options for what became known as Operation Neptune's Spear. Because the assault on the Abbottabad compound was to be a clandestine "deniable" operation with the chain of command running from the president through the Agency director to the JSOC commander, the planning for it took place within the Langley headquarters, not at Bagram or other SOF sites. Rehearsals, nevertheless, ensued at military bases. In the actual assault on the terrorist compound, the Agency sent an interpreter to accompany the SEALs on the raid helicopters.

After the announcement that Geronimo was an "EKIA" (Enemy Killed in Action), Leon Panetta stated during an interview that the mission was a Title 50 operation. By that statement, he made clear that it was a covert action and not a Title 10 regular military enterprise, which entailed a violation of Pakistani sovereignty with regular armed forces. Panetta explained that the raid was commanded by the president though Panetta as CIA director and carried out by the military officer in charge of the Joint Special Operations Command, Vice Admiral McRaven. As with many similar (although not as famous) covert actions, Panetta's explanation underscores the entwining of executive branch, the Central Intelligence Agency, and the Special Operations Forces that unfolded after September 11th.[35] The exemplary execution of the Abbottabad attack underscored the eroding walls separating the specialized military and intelligence communities within the American security apparatus that harkened back to the initial soldier-spy fusion by Nathan Hale during the American Revolutionary War.

Pursuing a shadowy terrorist threat since 9/11 has blurred the lines between intelligence gathering and soldiering in ways unimaginable in Nathan Hale's late-eighteenth-century world, however. Today's undercover military forces operate under legal codes normally promulgated for secret operatives. Moreover, present-day intelligence officers organize and train local personnel to fight like partisans, duties that unconventional special operators might routinely perform. The interchangeability of roles, in part, has also been evidenced recently in some top-level security appointments. Leon Panetta, who was CIA director from 2009 to 2011, moved to secretary of defense until his retirement in early 2013. General Petraeus, onetime CENTCOM commander and then ISAF head, moved into Panetta's job at the CIA from 2011 to 2012. While atop the Central Intelligence Agency, Petraeus oversaw a sharp escalation of the paramilitary Agency drone strikes in Pakistan and Yemen.

Additionally, the CIA added secret bases and case officers in Afghanistan to collect information for targeting Taliban and al Qaeda figures inside Pakistan. General Petraeus shifted troops into intelligence roles. When he was head of the U.S. Central Command, he reportedly signed a "classified order authorizing American Special Operations troops to collect intelligence in Saudi Arabia, Jordan, Iran, and other places outside traditional war zones."[36] This effort expanded SOF's now-standard practice of scooping up notebooks, computers, and storage devices during the course of their raids. It and similar intelligence-gathering efforts folded together the roles of the special warrior and field spy in a novel manner.

Even in undeclared war zones, the joint special warrior–spy fusion saw application. When the United States returned to focus on Somalia after the withdrawal in the wake of the 1993 Black Hawk Down incident, General McChrystal referred obliquely to the "small number of intelligence-collection assets" being necessary to target fugitive al Qaeda leaders on the run in the Horn of Africa country.[37] Other open sources describe the presence of the CIA field operatives in the Horn during the 1990s.[38] Somalia also witnessed SOF kinetic actions to kill al Qaeda–affiliated terrorists.[39]

With military and intelligence operators carrying out classified missions within the deadly pockets in Africa, Central Asia, and the Middle East, the sharp distinctions between them become blurry. The murkiness is no cause for alarm, however, for it mirrors the shadowiness of America's nonuniformed foes, who move almost seamlessly from combatant to noncombatant within the larger society after an ambush. These insurgent-terrorists simply cache their weapons and melt into the population to strike another day. The very nature of elusive terrorists dictates a shadowy counterterrorist response. It is a murky battlefield, one where combatants do not necessarily wear uniforms, display insignia, and carry arms openly, as prescribed by the Geneva Conventions for regular armies.

chapter seven

SOF–CIA in Somalia, Yemen, and Beyond

THE LUSTER surrounding the dramatic assault on the planet's most notorious terrorist in Abbottabad did not fade, but the denouement it presumed never materialized. Bin Laden's departure from this world delivered no collapse of al Qaeda Central or its affiliates. In some respects, al Qaeda's predominant role as terrorist headquarters had already diminished by the time of bin Laden's demise. It served increasingly as an inspirer and symbolizer rather than as a coordinating center of international terrorism. The counterterror campaign that Osama bin Laden's bloody deeds sparked has by necessity opened more fronts, even with his passing. The terror home office stayed fixed along the Afghan-Pakistan borderlands, but it recognized aspiring franchisees in Yemen, Somalia, Algeria, Libya, Nigeria, Mali, Syria, and back again in Iraq with a vengeance. Even so, al Qaeda Central was eclipsed by other sinister terrorist networks, as will be examined. Thus, the arch-terrorist's elimination, in fact, brought no slackening in counterterrorism operations or in U.S. military deployments, however limited in scope, in emerging jihadi venues.

Besides, the United States never fully pressed ahead robustly with a well-resourced strategy to root out terrorist movements. Washington's most egregious backward step took place in Iraq when President Obama ordered the withdrawal of all U.S. combat forces from the Persian Gulf nation by the end of 2011. At that time, peace had nearly been restored by American military forces after the carnage that began in the wake of the U.S.-led intervention in 2003. Inauspiciously, America's military withdrawal coincided with a historic political upsurge in the lands bordering Iraq. As the Middle East convulsed in antiauthoritarian revolutions known as the Arab Spring, several governments in the region collapsed, opening their territory to jihadi networks. Libya, Egypt, Yemen, and Syria plunged into instability and bloodshed as violent extremist movements took root amid political unrest. The most menacing terrorist group emerged in Syria from remnants of the AQI movement, which moved to a new front within the Syrian chaos.

Under the leadership of Abu Bakr al Baghdadi, the old AQI franchise metamorphosed into a vicious killing machine in the name of radicalized Islam. Now known as the Islamic State of Iraq and Syria, the terrorist network burst into international prominence for its grisly beheadings of hostages and brutal rule in conquered territories.[1] After its thrust back into Iraq from its Syrian stronghold, ISIS (also known as the Islamic State in Iraq and the Levant, or ISIL) proclaimed a caliphate to replace the one lost after World War I. Al Baghdadi, a former religious scholar, proclaimed himself the caliph of the Islamic State in late June 2014. The astounding success of the Islamic State in carving out microstates in Syria and Iraq quickly generated imitators elsewhere. Jihadis in Libya, Yemen, Somalia, and Sinai raised the black banner of ISIS and declared their militias as "provinces" of the Islamic State. They also presented a challenge to the West and its Middle Eastern allies.

Not insignificantly, the evolving counterterrorist-insurgency strategy forged and refined in the Iraqi and Afghan theaters offered several guideposts for similar conflicts today and tomorrow. One early instance of the decade-long growing coordination between SOF and the CIA outside the two wartime theaters took place in Yemen, which soon blinked on Washington radar screens as a terrorist haven after the 9/11 attacks. By early 2002, small numbers of SOF troops were working with an Agency team in Sana'a, the country's capital. America's second lethal drone strike (the first killed was al Qaeda's number three, Mohammad Atef) occurred in Yemen against Abu Ali al-Harithi, the mastermind of the USS *Cole* bombing in 2000. The ISA tracked al-Harithi's cell phone and monitored his travel in a Toyota 4x4 some one hundred miles east of Sana'a on November 3, 2002. The ISA communicated its intelligence to the Agency, which commanded some of the drones flying over Yemen. A CIA Predator fired a Hellfire missile into al-Harithi's vehicle, killing him and five other militants after a nine-month manhunt.

The handoff of ISA information to the CIA for the "kill" exemplified another variation of military-intelligence unity. In this case, military intelligence officials did the collecting and analyzing of information, and civilian operatives executed the direct-action operation against the target. This constituted a role reversal of sorts. Usually, intelligence flowed from the civilian Agency to the specialized units for execution. The intelligence-military cooperation had now become a two-way street. The Pentagon transferred the ISA from the U.S. Intelligence and Security Command to JSOC in 2006.[2] This change enhanced JSOC's tactical intelligence capacity, but the special operations headquarters continued to work closely with the spy agency.

Distant from the main combat theaters in Afghanistan and the Levant, Somalia was something of a backwater to CENTCOM. It never dispatched U.S. ground forces again to the ungoverned country after President Clinton withdrew all American troops in 1995, a year and a half after the Black Hawk Down incident. Other foreign contingents and aid workers, who served under UN auspices, also abandoned what most observers regarded as the world's poorest country. The Horn of Africa nation tumbled into chaos and violence shortly after the ouster of its long-time military dictator, Mohamed Said Barre, in 1991. The passage of time witnessed no amelioration in the intervening years. Its lawlessness offered a permissive environment for jihadis, some of whom were involved in the twin terrorist attacks on the American embassies in Nairobi and Dar es Salaam in 1998. A few years later, in 2002, Kenya was the scene of an attack on the Paradise Hotel and a ground-to-air missile firing that narrowly failed to down an Israeli airliner. These Islamist assaults emanated from Somalia. Not until the 9/11 terrorism, nevertheless, did Washington home in on the Horn of Africa as threat to the United States.

In June 2002, the Pentagon set up the Combined Joint Task Force—Horn of Africa in the tiny country of Djibouti, which fronts onto the Red Sea just where it opens into the Gulf of Aden. Its proximity to Yemen and the Indian Ocean also gives it a strategic location. With less than a million inhabitants, the former French Somalia boasted a decrepit military base, into which the Pentagon poured millions of dollars to fortify and recondition. Fort Lemonier opened its gates eventually to some four thousand U.S. troops and other personnel, as well as to a French Foreign Legion brigade. The former French outpost also hosted elements from JSOC and the CIA's CTC, who kept watchful eyes on the Horn and the Arabian Peninsula.

Even with a U.S. military installation in Djibouti, the Bush administration chose to wage its Somali counterterrorist campaign in the shadows, relying on JSOC and the CIA, with the intelligence operatives in the lead.[3] The two security branches hunted about twenty al Qaeda terrorists. The CIA paid Somali warlords to kill or capture the al Qaeda fugitives who slipped between Kenya and Somalia. Those terrorist suspects taken into CIA custody were transported by the Agency to secret "black sites," or prisons, run in Afghanistan, Egypt, Morocco, and other countries for enhanced interrogations. Local threats also emerged with the formation of Somali Islamic extremist groups. The al Shabaab movement, a militant wing of the Council of Islamic Courts, came to dominate most of the southern region of the country in the second half of 2006. It lost little time in making threats against the West. Al Shabaab's sudden takeover disrupted the CIA's warlord strategy for apprehending al Qaeda figures. The warlords fell to the tender mercies of the new Islamist overlords in the sun-blasted country. Nor could the CIA field officers safely conduct their agent-handling business in the violent Islamist-dominated landscape.

In the main, Washington coped with the al Shabaab danger by relying on Ethiopia, which in 2006 militarily swept al Shabaab from Mogadishu before its invasion set off a widespread anti-Ethiopian insurgency. Along with modest air support of ground operations, JSOC personnel assisted Addis Ababa by advising as well as passing intelligence to the Ethiopian army. This force pushed the Islamist militias out of the capital and into a southeastern pocket of Somalia.[4] Later, the United States recruited and backed the African Union to handle its Somali problem. The continental-wide organization established the African Union Mission in Somalia (AMISOM) to police the strife-filled country.

AMISOM deployed several thousand troops from member states, including Kenya and Uganda, which retook the capital and backed the Western-oriented transitional federal government's tenuous grip on most of the country. The AMISOM peacekeepers managed to elbow the al Shabaab militants into the country's southeast quadrant, which made Somalia safer, but it contributed to insecurity in Kenya. Al Shabaab unleashed terrorist attacks on the Kenyan people, including the mass-casualty assault on Nairobi's posh Westgate Mall in 2013. Despite its occasional terrorism inside Mogadishu, however, al Shabaab no longer controlled the capital city.

Washington turned again to JSOC and the CIA to hunt down al Qaeda and its associates aligned with al Shabaab operating in the Horn of Africa. General McChrystal enacted in Somalia a similar coordination scheme as used in other terrorist havens. Just as he gave overwatch in Iraq to the Delta Force and overwatch in Afghanistan to SEAL's Team 6 and the 75th Ranger Regiment (code-named Red), he placed Task Force Orange over the Horn.[5] The expanded intelligence gathering enabled the Special Operations Forces to target high-level militants.

Among the early aerial attacks, a U.S. Tomahawk missile fired from a warship off the Somali coast took the life of Aden Hashi Ayro, who had been tracked for weeks in 2008, not long after Washington declared al Shabaab an international terrorist group. Ayro was an al Qaeda functionary thought to be the architect of al Shabaab suicide bombings all across the country and the murderer of a BBC journalist.[6] Another strike took down Saleh Ali Saleh Nabhan, who had been tracked in East Africa by the CIA and JSOC for six years. In September 2009, JSOC Little Bird helicopters flying from a warship off the Somali coast had the senior al Qaeda figure in its crosshairs after intelligence personnel located and then predicted Nabhan's travel route. After the lead helicopter fired its machine guns at the speeding vehicle to kill its occupants, SEAL Team 6 members landed and collected DNA specimens and information carried by the four corpses, one of which was Nabhan.[7]

The heightening dangers posed by al Shabaab to East Africa resulted in JSOC setting up clandestine subbases in Kismayo and Baledogle, the former in the south along the Kenya border and the latter about seventy miles northwest of Mogadishu. Each hosted fewer than fifty military personnel, who concentrated on locating al Shabaab leaders and al Qaeda renegades. They also coordinated with the Counterterrorism Center in Langley to overwatch the volatile Horn of Arica region.[8] The small SOF footprints were part of the broader Somali-American campaign to capture or kill known jihadis in the area by fixing their position and then finishing them. A top-level al Qaeda–linked operative, Ahmed Abdi Godane, who led the al Shabaab group, fell victim to the enhanced JSOC-CTC capabilities within Somalia. Godane had long been associated with other Islamists movements before taking command of al Shabaab. His end came from a Hellfire missile fired in September 2014. Thus, the SOF-CIA synchronization honed elsewhere was adaptable to different human and geographical terrains.

During the first half of the 2000s, when the United States was preoccupied with the fighting in Iraq and Afghanistan, Yemen drew fewer U.S. resources. Besides, its autocratic ruler, Ali Abdullah Saleh, seemed firmly in control of the water-starved, impoverished Arabian nation. As the years passed, Yemen aroused deeper apprehension with the growing presence of al Qaeda in the Arabian Peninsula (AQAP). JSOC participated with the CIA in an interagency team overseen by the U.S. ambassador to the Arabian Peninsula country. Special Forces troops trained Yemeni antiterrorism units. JSOC conducted most of the first lethal operations against AQAP from its base across the Gulf of Aden in Djibouti. The Yemeni authorities took credit for the aircraft and drone attacks on antigovernment militants, a claim that cloaked the strikes behind a thin official veil. The Djibouti government, on the other hand, demanded the right of approval for any lethal missions launched from its Fort Lemonier. The Pentagon worked out a satisfactory agreement with Djibouti that addressed its concerns.

In 2011, the White House switched the targeting assignment against Anwar al-Awlaki from the U.S. military to the CIA. By that time, the CIA had completed a secret drone base within Saudi Arabia. The Agency enjoyed long and discreet relations with the desert kingdom, enabling it to conduct sensitive operations from its sands into Yemen. The spies also acquired a reputation for more accuracy than their military counterparts. In addition, the spy agency had sources within AQAP relaying pinpoint targeting information for drone missiles strikes. The handoff from JSOC to the CIA went without a hitch or even a murmur of public dissent. The Pentagon, indeed, transferred eight drones to the CIA inventory. All the while, the Defense Department broadened its footprint with more drones and enhanced bases in Ethiopia, Djibouti, Kenya, and the Seychelles. The Pentagon also operated drones during the brief NATO-led intervention into Libya in the first half of 2011. The Central Intelligence Agency, for its part, managed the drone war in Pakistan that, as yet, it still does not publicly acknowledge. One author wrote that the military-to-intelligence handover resembled the collaboration in the bin Laden raid in that it constituted "a near-seamless integration of counterterrorism operations between the military and the CIA."[9] Much the same could be said about other operations that linked the two communities.

The SOF-CIA collaboration in the country at the tip of the Arabian Peninsula deepened with the founding of the affiliate AQAP, which came about from splinter jihadi factions in 2009. AQAP aroused apprehensions from the inflammatory preaching of the American-born Anwar al-Awlaki. His online appeals for jihad, in part, motivated U.S. Army major Nidal Hasan to kill thirteen people at Fort Hood, Texas, and inspired Nigerian student Umar Farouk Abdulmutallab to attempt to blow up a Detroit-destined airline with a bomb in his underwear. Fears of further terrorism prompted the Obama administration to pull the trigger on Awlaki with a drone-fired missile in 2012. Afterward, Washington strengthened its involvement in Yemen out of concerns about AQAP's potential terrorist reach.

Not long after AQAP's founding, the United States stepped up its assistance to President Saleh, a former Yemini army general, to combat al Qaeda before it struck American targets. The Pentagon dispatched Special Operations Forces to train Yemeni security forces. Almost immediately, the U.S. military and CIA personnel were caught in a triangular conflict, because President Saleh had more than just al Qaeda as an enemy. In Yemen's northern quarter, the Houthis staged a rebellion against the central government in 2004. The Houthis had adopted the name of their onetime leader, Hussein al-Houthi, who led a mainly Zaidi sect (an offshoot from Shiite Islam). The Houthi rebels fought Saleh for their own autonomous homeland within Yemen. For its part, Washington tried to stay clear of the Houthi conflict and concentrate on al Qaeda. Moreover, the Obama administration strove to avoid a clash with the Iranian-backed Houthis because the White House sought a nuclear arms agreement with Iran. Fighting the Houthis' militias stood to jeopardize a deal. The White House restraint paid off for the administration when it concluded its nuclear weapons accord with Tehran in 2015. No similar restraint marked America's actions against AQAP. Operating from a secret base in Saudi Arabia, the CIA launched deadly drone missile strikes on several AQAP leaders as part of its counterterrorism response.

Things went from bad to worse in Yemen as the upheaval from the Arab Spring engulfed the already reeling country. Even though President Saleh had ruled for three decades, he succumbed to the turmoil rippling across the country. In 2012 he fled the country and turned over the reins of power to his vice president, Abed Rabbo Masour Hadi. But Hadi fared no better. In fact, he faced not only the onslaught of Houthi fighters and al Qaeda gunmen but also the volte-face of his former president. Saleh made common cause with the Houthis against his chosen successor in a desperate roll of the dice to return to power. Hadi took flight for safety in Saudi Arabia, where he persisted in plotting his own comeback to power.

So tumultuous had Yemen become that the Obama administration pulled out its diplomatic and security presence completely. It withdrew the U.S. Embassy staff, the CIA field operatives, and even, temporarily, the SOF troops in the spring of 2015. Yemen's political turbulence cast doubt on President Obama's counterterrorism strategy, which banked on air strikes, in-and-out raids by special mission units, and Special Forces advisers to professionalize indigenous security units. Its failure in the desiccated country raised questions of its successful application to uproot ISIS from large swaths of territory in Syria and Iraq.[10]

Meanwhile in Iraq, the JSOC-CIA strike duo again worked out an arrangement to confront a renewed threat once the regular U.S. military departed. Functioning like a wrestling tag team, the CIA replaced SOF in Iraq when circumstances dictated a substitution. The war-torn Gulf state suffered a resurgence of violence from jihadi terrorists and from the spillover of fighting in Syria in early 2012. Postoccupation Iraq requested U.S. assistance. As noted earlier, the United States had redeployed all its combat forces from Iraq in December 2011, except for a handful of military trainers and advisers. As terrorist attacks mounted afterward, the Baghdad government called for American help in combating the relentless bombings and killings. Prior to the official U.S. military withdrawal, SOF worked with Iraq's Counterterrorism Service (CTS) during much of the Iraq War. But in early 2012, the White House directed the CIA to assist the CTS. The CIA covert profile lent itself to a nonmilitary, low-visibility training program of Iraqi counterterrorism forces favored by the U.S. government. The Pentagon's mission transfer to the CIA complemented other Agency actions in the region.

Moving from an overt U.S. military presence to a covert CIA advising-and-assisting effort enabled America with reduced visibility to gradually strengthen Baghdad's counterterrorism effectiveness against resurging jihadi attacks. Reportedly reluctant to cease working with the CTS, the military and SOF, nevertheless, accepted the decision in the end, further downsizing its tiny contingent. Thus, they observed the CIA takeover of the collaboration with Iraq's CTS without a public feud.[11] The White House responded tepidly to the renewed terrorism within Iraq, believing that small covert Agency teams on their own were capable of stiffening Iraqi security forces against a rising tide of Sunni Islamist terrorism.

This strategy proved just a temporary fix, however, for events on the ground transformed Washington's perceptions and actions regarding Iraq. When ISIS rampaged across northern and western Iraq, the United States dropped its slender covert effort. The barbarous upsurge of terrorism perpetrated under the black ISIS flag during 2014 required repeated U.S. and allied air strikes and the reintroduction of more than 3,400 U.S. military personnel, including SOF and field intelligence officers, back into Iraq. A dramatic new scourge upended the neat transfer of security duties from the U.S. armed forces to the spy agency.

The emergence of ISIS as a full-blown Islamist terrorist threat transformed the Middle East. When ISIS overran about a third of Iraq, it carved out statelets in both Syria and Iraq in which it administered limited government services while repressing the local population with harsh treatment and religious orthodoxy. Washington reacted wanly to the Islamic State's astounding conquests. Gradually, it inserted CIA and SOF elements into Syria to complement its larger force within Iraq. The CIA interacted with so-called moderate Syrian rebel militias fighting the Bashar al-Assad regime while also countering the al Nusra Front, a group linked to al Qaeda. Agency field operatives trained, armed, and advised fighters against Damascus. The Pentagon training programs fell well short of even the CIA's modest efforts to turn out anti-Assad troops. Setbacks characterized the American mobilization projects, largely because most recruits viewed Bashar al-Assad as the main bête noire, not their fellow countrymen who joined up with radical Sunni Islamist militias.

One arena noteworthy because of success revolved around the combined JSOC-CIA campaign to locate and kill high-value al Nusra and Islamic State officials in Iraq and Syria. Like the fusion cells pioneered earlier in Iraq and Afghanistan, the United States formed clearinghouses for information from the Agency's CTC, NSA, and the National Geospatial-Intelligence Agency. The Pentagon lofted aircraft or drones with electronic devices overhead, enabling the National Security Agency to soak up electronic signals sent by militants on the ground. The CIA and the Defense Intelligence Agency beefed up recruiting of local sources from bordering countries to make up for the lack of U.S. intelligence officials on the ground, because there are no U.S. embassies or consulates to work out of within the Islamic State. American intelligence operatives also liaised closely with intelligence services in Jordan, Saudi Arabia, and the Kurdish provinces in Iraq. Electronic eavesdropping, overhead imagery, and social media analysis also helped U.S. manhunters zero in on senior Islamic State figures.

Drone strikes—separate from CENTCOM's regular aerial bombing campaign—killed several Islamic State leaders. Two top figures in the al Qaeda–linked Khorasan Group, which plotted attacks on the United States, met death in the summer of 2015; they were Muhsin al-Fadhli, the group leader, and David Drugeon, a skilled French bomb maker. The Islamic State's deputy, Haji Mutazz, suffered a similar fate around the same time. Unlike in Pakistan and Yemen, where the CIA fired the drone missiles, JSOC operatives pulled the trigger on the air strikes in Syria and Iraq, reportedly because the Obama administration preferred that the military handle lethal operations rather than civilian intelligence officials. This procedure necessitated tight collaboration between the Agency's Counterterrorism Center and the Joint Special Operations Command.[12] The terrorist takedown operations were intended to throw the jihadi leadership off stride. By themselves, the aerial killing missions could not defeat the Islamic State, as new leaders replaced the fallen.

Washington's containment strategy of the Islamic State came under intense scrutiny in the wake of the multipronged terrorist attack in Paris on November 13, 2015, when 130 concert goers, café customers, and other innocents were gunned down and murdered by a Belgium-based jihadi cell with ISIS ties. During an interview just hours before terrorists struck on Parisian streets, President Obama asserted that "we have contained" the Islamic State.[13] In response to the Paris attacks, and other recent acts of terrorism, the Obama administration decided to bolster America's SOF presence in Iraq, together with fifty special operators already committed to Syria a month earlier to organize Kurdish and Sunni Arab forces.

Ordered by the White House, the Pentagon scrambled to field more than a one-hundred-member intelligence and strike force to Iraq. Making the announcement, Ashton Carter, the secretary of defense, referred not to JSOC but to a "specialized expeditionary targeting force to assist Iraq and Kurdish Peshmerga forces," in keeping with the Defense Department's nondisclosure of the secretive command.[14] As with the stepped-up U.S. commitment to the Syrian front against ISIS, the new detachment designated for Iraqi duty had advise-and-assist tasks. Apart from the forces assigned to close-in combat, this new team comprised personnel to perform intelligence gathering and analysis. The Pentagon inserted these elite manhunting forces to track down and capture or kill high-value ISIS targets. By accumulating intelligence from ISIS prisoners, SOF could create "a virtuous cycle of better intelligence, which generates more targets, more raids, and more momentum," in the words of the Pentagon chief in his testimony before the House Armed Services Committee, where he announced White House strategy.[15]

The expeditionary contingent relied on techniques perfected earlier in Iraq and Syria. CIA case officers and JSOC intelligence specialists had to overcome the lack of embassies and diplomatic cover to cultivate local sources for information. They resorted to other espionage methods for human intelligence. Uniformed and plainclothes intelligence officers, as noted above, learned to utilize local informers from nearby countries to relay information about the whereabouts of high-value Islamic State leaders. They also used signals intelligence to geo-locate the bad guys in denied areas. As for intelligence-driven raids, the Pentagon had in mind the type of operation that came to light about a combat action in May 2015. Delta Force operators snuck across the Iraqi border into Syria in Black Hawk helicopters and V-22 Osprey aircraft and descended on the town of Amr, close to Deir al-Zour, to surround the residence of Abu Sayyaf, an associate of ISIS chieftain Abu Bakr al Baghdadi. Identified as a key facilitator for oil and gas sales by the Islamic State, Sayyaf oversaw illicit financial transactions that brought cash into the terrorist outfit. Although Sayyaf died in a fierce gunfight, he left behind a rich haul of information in recovered cell phones, laptops, and paper documents. His wife, Umm Sayyaf, was captured and later interrogated because she also was an ISIS member.[16] Intelligence collection enterprises had definitely become part of SOF's repertoire.

Beyond the Somali, Iraqi, and Syrian conflict zones, the Special Operations Forces have played a leading part in training African armies in counterinsurgency to combat the threats of violent extremism as terrorist movements sought to carve out safe havens in failing states. SOF worked in Mali, Chad, and Libya in training missions. Separately, the White House also dispatched some one hundred Special Forces soldiers in 2011 to Central Africa to assist local forces in Uganda, the Central African Republic, and the Democratic Republic of Congo to track down the notorious bandit leader Joseph Kony, who headed the Lord's Resistance Army that pillaged, murdered, raped, and abducted about seventy thousand children into its ranks while internally displacing an estimated two million people. The small U.S. special contingent worked to help African soldiers in their push to locate the brutal warlord. They were banned from firing their weapons unless in self-defense. In short, their role was advisory, not combatant.

Trying to replicate the tight SOF-CIA coordination beyond Iraq, Afghanistan, and Yemen, JSOC set up a task force near the

Pentagon. The Joint Special Operations Task Force—National Capital Region (JSOTF-NCR) focused on breaking down barriers between its teammate agencies within the American government. The JSOTF-NCR copied the model used abroad by assembling representatives from the CIA, NSA, FBI, and the National Media Exploitation Center together with SOF. The National Media Exploitation Center downloaded and extracted names, telephone numbers, images, and messages from computers, CDs, and thumb drives. This information was processed, stored, and related to other data so as to zero in on individuals and networks to identify them to JSOC.[17] The symbiotic linkage between special warriors and elite spies notched closer just outside the nation's capital. Built on the effective models in terrorist theaters, the JSOTF-NCR concentrated on emerging militant havens in the earth's remote corners.

The close SOF-CIA alignment in countering the spread of al Qaeda branches went forward despite the winding down of the wars in Iraq and in Afghanistan. One journalistic account said that the "kind of seamless operational cooperation [between SOF, CIA, DIA, NSA, and FBI] became common on a smaller scale in Yemen, Pakistan, and other shadowy battlegrounds."[18] Media reports have also referred to both special force members and Agency operatives in the new battlegrounds of Africa and the Middle East. For instance, one newspaper reported that the CIA "forged a good relationship with its counterparts in Algeria."[19] Earlier, Algeria came close to being ruled by an Islamist movement, which the government suppressed in a bloody insurgency during the early 1990s, rendering the North African country receptive to intelligence sharing vis-à-vis radical Islamist groups.

Twin factors led the United States to create a string of counterterrorism hubs in the Middle East, Africa, and Southwest Asia in the manner pioneered by President Bush with SOF bases in

Djibouti and Mindanao. First, the enduring consolidation of the Islamic State within Iraq and Syria induced copycat groups elsewhere to swear their loyalty to Abu Bakr al Baghdadi as Caliph Ibrahim. At least eight militant groups pledged their loyalty to the ISIS leader, whose group eclipsed al Qaeda under Ayman al-Zawahiri (who replaced Osama bin Laden). These subgroups regarded themselves as "provinces" of the caliphate seated in Raqqa, Syria. Like their parent network, they spawned murder, mayhem, and totalitarian rule of Sharia law. The second factor arose with the terrorist attack in Paris on November 13, 2015, and other, almost simultaneous carnages in Beirut, Lebanon, and Nigeria. The Parisian murders by suicidal gunmen in the very heart of Western Europe galvanized popular opinion in the Euro-Atlantic world to thwart the rising menace. Three weeks later, an ISIS-inspired married couple killed fourteen people in San Bernardino, California. Public and congressional pressure built within the United States for the Obama administration to go on the offensive against ISIS and its acolytes. To address the accumulating terrorist threat, the United States doubled down on the tactics employed in Afghanistan, Iraq, Syria, and Somalia.

The Pentagon's new basing plan for sites staffed by SOF teams laid out four hubs (which incorporated those already up and running in Afghanistan and Djibouti) and four smaller and more basic installations, referred to as "spokes," in such countries as Nigeria and Cameroon. Military personnel in these outposts range from five hundred to five thousand members to engage in "crisis response, counterterrorism, or strikes on high-value targets," according to Ashton Carter. The defense secretary added: "Because we cannot predict the future, these regional nodes—from Morón, Spain, to Jalalabad, Afghanistan—will provide forward presence to respond to a range of crises, terrorist and other kinds."[20] Once again, pushback for JSOC's outward reach came not from the CIA but rather the State Department, which "warned about the creeping militarization of American foreign policy."[21] It reacted to the eagerness of foreign governments in non-Western countries to cultivate tighter relationships with the Pentagon in return for military assistance. In sum, the new redoubts are seen as places to collect intelligence and conduct counterstrikes against ISIS tentacles. As such, they perpetuated the close-knit alignment between SOF and intelligence operatives begun ardently in the Balkans and deepened after the 9/11 terrorist attacks.

Partnership and the Use of Drones

Another dimension in the decades-long SOF-CIA partnership involved the business of remotely piloted aircraft, known commonly as drones. Both security communities ran drone operations to monitor and to strike ground targets. Over time, senior White House officials worked out a modus vivendi that has enabled warriors and spies to control and to employ drones against Islamist militants. The CIA-directed drone strikes were generally carried out in Pakistan and Yemen. The Special Operations Forces conducted unmanned air strikes in Afghanistan as part of the Pentagon's overall war effort. They also executed limited aerial attacks in Somalia, for that kinetic program was much more restricted than elsewhere. As noted above, JSOC and the CIA shifted roles in Yemen, with the spy agency taking over the air-to-ground campaign after some military mishaps. The Pentagon facilitated the transfer by turning over armed drones in its inventory to the Agency. No evidence became public of any bureaucratic infighting over the new alignment between the two communities.

President Bush initiated targeted drone strikes against difficult-to-reach al Qaeda fugitives responsible for the skiff explosion against the USS *Cole* and the massive terrorism on September 11th. When President Obama settled into the White House, he greatly accelerated a drone-centric counterterrorism campaign, particularly in Pakistan, where al Qaeda and Taliban figures sheltered from the insurgency across the border in Afghanistan. Air strikes, in fact, assumed a central role in the president's tripartite counterterrorism strategy, along with SOF commando raids and partnerships with local forces against Islamist militias.

President Obama's repeated drone killings became a core element in his counterterrorism strategy against al Qaeda. Shortly after Osama bin Laden's death, the administration concluded that its drone air strikes had degraded the parent network's operational capacity. Top security officials testified to Congress and spoke publicly to the media. American counterterrorism operations opened "an important window of vulnerability for the core al-Qaeda organization in Pakistan and Afghanistan," in the words of David H. Petraeus, then CIA director. Michael G. Vickers, the undersecretary of defense for intelligence, speculated that "within 18 to 24 months, core al-Qaeda's cohesion and operational capabilities could be degraded to the point that the group could fragment." In other testimony, Director of National Intelligence James R. Clapper Jr. underscored the upbeat assessments, due in part to the spy agencies' improvement in sharing information and working coordinate operations against terrorist networks.[22] These postmortems turned out to be woefully premature; they were also too fixated on al Qaeda as the alpha and omega of all Islamist terrorism.

For the past few years, Obama's use of "killer drones" to neutralize jihadis has come under sharp criticism for several reasons.[23]

Intelligence purists contended that the Central Intelligence Agency has lost its traditional focus on gathering and analyzing information. Hence, the concentration on the aerial assassinations of terrorists, no matter how threatening to the U.S. homeland, transformed the Agency into a killing machine and a covert training program for counterinsurgents. Thus, air strikes and paramilitary operations have taken the spy agency off point. As result, the CIA has paid insufficient attention to the rise and arming of China, the resurgence of Russia, the nuclear ambitions of Iran, and other national security flash points. The classified findings of Obama's own President's Intelligence Advisory Board drew congressional rebuke and demands for a return focus on conventional perils.[24]

CIA officials replied that abundant resources were, in fact, still committed to classic espionage subjects. They averred that the buildup of the Counterterrorism Center had not been at the expense of old-line concerns. After the 9/11 terrorism, the CTC went from some three hundred personnel to around two thousand, which represented one in ten Agency employees. John O. Brennan, the CIA director after March 2013, testified before Congress during his confirmation hearings that the scope of the Silent Service's involvement in the lethality business was an "aberration from its traditional role." But he made it clear that Langley would not relinquish its fleet of armed drones. The nation's top spy stated that the agency "must continue to be able to provide the president with this option."[25] Since Brennan's candid answer, he did preside over some shifting in the CIA drone actions, as noted in the conflict with the Islamic State.

Other CIA detractors also held that the drone campaign against extremists militarized the Agency. They have argued against the "bureaucratization of the CIA's paramilitary killing program" because of legal and moral objections rather than issues of interdepartmental rivalries with the Pentagon. Indeed, much of the criticism of the CIA-overseen drone campaign centers on Pakistan and Yemen, which have witnessed the lion's share of aerial missile firings from armed drones.[26] Ironically, the United States was—and is—not at war with either nation. Since drone missile strikes have become prevalent in both countries, some opponents argued that the Pentagon should take over the missions instead of the CIA, thinking that the military's hand would be more transparent and subject to more legislative oversight than Langley's quasi-secret air war. Indeed, off-loading targeted killings to the military will add requirements that the Agency is not bound by in laws and practices. Former California congresswoman Jane Harman advocated a special drone court to review and authorize drone strikes and proposed that "all sustained drone and cyberattacks should be conducted by Department of Defense agencies."[27]

Civil libertarians, on the other hand, posited that the transfer of drone-killing operations from a civilian department to a military one made no difference in the legal and moral realm. Killings from the skies, in this judgment, were illegal and ethically wrong without the due process of a jury trial, forensic evidence, and legal defense of the accused. The controversial air strike on the AQAP propagandist in Yemen particularly called into question the drone operations because it killed Anwar al-Awlaki, who, as noted earlier, was an American citizen. Born in the state of New Mexico, Awlaki underwent Islamist radicalization and traveled to Yemen. There he publicly took up arms against his former homeland by inciting terrorist violence in his online broadcasts and writings. As previously mentioned, U.S. army major Nidal Malik Hassan, who carried out the Fort Hood murders in 2009, drew inspiration from Awlaki's Islamist teachings. In effect, Awlaki renounced his citizenship by his traitorous behavior and invited his own death by warring against his former homeland.

The news media widely reported that SOF and the CIA maintained separate lists for possible drone strikes inside Yemen. Initially, JSOC drew a bead on Awlaki four months before his death, but the AQAP chief managed to escape the missiles fired from drones and Marine Harrier jets. David Petraeus, then at the CIA, ordered the transfer of several drones from Pakistan to a secret CIA base in Saudi Arabia. Next, the White House reassigned the Awlaki hunt to the CIA, whose drones ultimately killed the terrorist inciter.[28] The controversy overhanging Awlaki's death had much to do with the fact that he was an American citizen who had been neither charged officially nor found guilty in a court trial. The secrecy veiling the decision to kill the AQAP chief sparked an uproar among human-rights advocates. Polls, however, show—then and now—overwhelming support among American voters for the drone policy. The public's approval cared nothing about which entity—SOF or CIA—pushed the missile-fire button.

Neither security community had a monopoly on errors in drone operations. In Yemen, JSOC mistakenly bombed a wedding party, killing many attendees. The CIA errantly struck and killed an Italian hostage and an American hostage, Giovanni Lo Porto and Warren Weinstein, respectively, in Pakistan in January 2015. Both men were aid workers taken prisoner and killed in an air strike on four al Qaeda operatives in the same building. Above all other nations, Pakistan was ground zero of more drone attacks, numbering more than four hundred in its tribal lands since 2004. The peak number of attacks came in late 2010, with more than twenty strikes in one month. More than 250 Pakistani civilians died as the result of drone bombardments within the lawless tribal belt along the Afghan border, many because of collateral damage, meaning they were too near the intended drone target and were caught in the explosive blast. Others died because, unlike other countries, the United States allows "signature strikes" on individuals in Pakistan, which are based on patterns of behavior, such as carrying a rifle. Thus, the actual identities of the targets are unknown. Elsewhere, the White House required confirming information about the intended drone victims. This often entailed lengthy drone surveillance, cell phone fixes, or other electronic sensor data as well as on-the-ground sources.[29]

The clamor from rights advocates is related to the Defense Department because it deepened calls for the CIA to turn over its drone operations to the Pentagon. Critics of the CIA drone attacks and its paramilitary operations argued that these activities are acts of war. Therefore, they "would best be carried out by military forces and subjected to the review and disclosure of other military operations." This line of argument also posited that the CIA "should be refocused on the job of intelligence collection."[30] The debate about the CIA's proper operational niche has a long history and dates to its founding in 1947. Should it be confined exclusively to gathering and analyzing intelligence? Alternatively, should it be given, as its empowering legislation states, other presidentially assigned operations?[31] Or should it maintain flexibility in waging the counterterrorism campaign?

Neat organizational charts, clear lines of authority, and straight stovepipes hold an appeal in an untidy world. Organizationally, good fences may make good neighbors, as Robert Frost famously wrote, but bureaucratic walls can impede cooperation, information sharing, and mutual load-bearing arrangements. Rigidly separate outfits often breed parochialism, which curtails or restricts interaction. Fighting in the shadows against a spectral-like foe demands not only adaptability but also multiple options from which policy makers can draw. There are circumstances where civilian intelligence field personnel afford the United States a low-visibility instrument for paramilitary missions. Other contingencies require the larger, more powerful SOF for behind-enemy-lines operations as well as direct-action assaults. On balance, the close SOF-CIA interaction, flourishing since the 9/11 attacks, has eroded al Qaeda's ranks and kept America safer. In the aftermath of the Islamic State's offensive into northern Iraq, the two U.S. security communities have escalated their operations into Syria and Iraq to combat the Islamist network. The tensions and low-level bickering between the two entities have been transitory (often confined to individual personalities rather than the overall communities) and nondisruptive to the larger strategy.

Following the 9/11 attacks, the "eyes" and "dagger" communities undertook joint covert operations that contributed to bridging their differences. Their missions fostered mutual dependency by linking intelligence with operational outcomes. Familiarity in this case, moreover, has not bred contempt but rather understanding. If anything, the operational side and the intelligence side learned to think like the other community. Admiral Eric Olson, former USSOCOM commander, noted that "field attitudes" contributed to good working relations between special warriors and agency officials. Having first worked together in Afghanistan, Iraq, or an undeclared war zone, the operators and case officers often again served together elsewhere, easing their relations.[32]

The CIA's National Clandestine Service hired many former SOF operators, facilitating understanding and cooperation because the soldiers-turned-case officers were familiar with how their former units conducted themselves in given operations. Another factor working to minimize potential rivalries stemmed from the Obama administration's high level of budgetary and political support for both communities. According to Michael Hayden, a

U.S. Air Force general (retired) who once headed both the NSA and the CIA, the potential feuding over the application of the Title 10 or Title 50 authorities never really materialized as an operational factor after the 9/11 attacks. The heads of the respective communities often conferred over which security agency was best suited to carry out a particular mission or function rather than trying to elbow aside the other.[33] Admiral Olson, who commanded USSOCOM during the Abbottabad operation, stated that "sometimes the edges of the authorities were fused together."[34] Still, he favored an effort to clear up ambiguities and overlaps that might harm the future effectiveness of SOF-CIA coordination.[35]

News reports of the "expanding netherworld between intelligence and military operations" confirm the twining of security agencies, where military and Agency personnel are nearly indistinguishable in the field. Their commingling at tucked-away bases has become so complete that one official back from Afghanistan argued: "You couldn't tell the difference between CIA officers, Special Forces guys, and contractors. They're all three blended together."[36]

Nor has the street been just one way, with information flowing from spy to warrior. A division of labor arose because of the nature of an overt war in Afghanistan and a covert campaign in Pakistan, which is not an authorized war zone. For the drone campaign inside Pakistan, which the CIA oversees, JSOC has furnished intelligence from captured, interrogated, and sometimes turned Taliban prisoners. At Bagram Air Base, where JSOC debriefs Taliban detainees, a trove of human intelligence is collected and evaluated. Some of the information aids in the precise targeting of Taliban militants in Pakistani villages or houses. Turned over to the CIA, the intelligence often triggered air strikes from lurking Predators and Reapers. Inside Afghanistan, the military usually took the lead, and the CIA reportedly saw itself in a support role. According to one media report, JSOC and CENTCOM generally enjoyed more freedom of action for its military operations. On the other hand, the CIA, with its deadly targeting of militants in Pakistan and Yemen, "is more centralized and run from Washington."[37]

Nonetheless, changes within the American security architecture are afoot. The CIA's role in the deadly drone program in Yemen and Pakistan has run into a buzz saw of political opposition from domestic and international critics. These detractors contend that the CIA strikes against terrorists circumvent lawful U.S. procedures, particularly when American citizens, such as Anwar al-Awlaki, fall victim to deadly missile strikes. The targeted killings have come to define a new American way of war in the eyes of its skeptics. They argue that it blurs the line between soldiers and spies, along with short-circuiting U.S. jurisprudence and international norms by which America has conducted warfare in its past. Human rights advocates state that some drone strikes are tantamount to extrajudicial killings—executions without trial. Congressional representatives accuse the White House of resorting to easy killings in lieu of legally fraught incarceration and interrogation. After the CIA overseas prisons (some called "black sites") were closed down and the transfer of terror suspects to Guantanamo Bay, Cuba, was halted, the critics charged that the Obama administration lacked an alternative. So it adopted the lines of least resistance; it opted for lethal force via drones to deal with militants rather than become entangled in convoluted legalities and in searches for jails to imprison them.[38]

A few years ago, the Obama administration signaled plans to scale down or remove the CIA from the U.S. drone campaign, a move that would hold substantial implications for the SOF-CIA relationship. It has expressed a "preference" for the military to take over the targeted-killing mission. The White House has already laid the groundwork in Yemen for shifting the drone operations from the spy agency to the Defense Department. The administration has also hinted at a return of the CIA to spying and strategic analysis.[39] Transferring the CIA's lethal drone program to the Pentagon would entail significant ramifications for not only the spy service but also the counterterrorism program.

In some sense, the drone controversy serves as a proxy for a much larger issue. There is criticism of the CIA's "supporting" role to the military's "supported" status. Detractors point to the two largest CIA stations since the Vietnam War being established in the war theaters of Iraq and Afghanistan. They argue that the Agency's Office of Military Affairs (created in 1992 after problems in the Gulf War) facilitated an excessive concentration on military intelligence for the counterterrorism campaign. All these steps have diverted the CIA from devoting resources and analysis away from its highest priority of "support to the policymaker" while it focused on the "military customer."[40]

Established by Ronald Reagan back in 1986, the CIA's Counterterrorism Center has played an outsized role in pulling together actionable intelligence for SOF and other security agencies since the 9/11 attacks. The CTC maintains intelligence subcenters in Pakistan, Iraq, and other locations, which feed information and analysis to the military for direct-action operations. Besides gathering and evaluating intelligence, the CIA picked up clandestine missions to train, equip, and advise indigenous forces, much as it did before and during the Vietnam War. Purists within the intelligence community have looked askance at these paramilitary programs. They believe that they distract the Agency from its traditional and primary intelligence mission. From time to time, congressional figures and CIA officials have advocated returning the Agency to its core intelligence functions.[41]

Proposed plans for reorientation of the spy agency entail the elimination or reduction of its paramilitary tasks, such as vetting, training, arming, and guiding allied security forces in Afghanistan, Syria, Iraq, and elsewhere. Only time will tell what, if any, changes come about within Langley's operations. Its attention for more than a decade has been focused on the terror threat. The CIA's relationships with other spy agencies around the world are also based on countering terrorism. Thus, a return to traditional threats as in the Cold War entails an enormous undertaking that might take years to effect. The full implications of such a course can only be hinted at now. On the surface, a bowing out of the CTC from its cloak-and-dagger operations necessitates a counterbalancing step up in the Pentagon's activities to take up the resulting slack. Offices within the Pentagon favor revamping the counterterrorism architecture to include a greater military role for amassing its own information to tackle the spreading terrorist threat.

Recommendations

This narrative's theme is that SOF and the CIA have drawn closer together and worked harmoniously in most instances to combat violent Islamists. Specific recommendations, nonetheless, can facilitate and ensure continued smooth and fruitful SOF-CIA interactions.[42] These recommendations include the following:

- The agencies should never be complacent, as interagency links, like international alliances, need constant attention, cultivation, and management.

- Rather than waiting until the last minute, the agencies should include relevant personnel from SOF and the CIA in the planning and assessment phase leading to each mission because such inclusion fosters cooperation.[43]
- Where and when it is not already being done, CIA experts "should be integrated into the military's training exercises and planning."[44]
- Coordination and consultation between SOF-CIA operatives on the tactical as well as operational level by their respective combatant commanders should be mandatory, while each maintains its separate line of authority.[45]
- SOF-CIA integrated operations must not diminish the distinct capabilities that each brings to the fight, unlikely as that may seem, given their unique cultures, operational modes, informational sources, and command structures.
- The end of the large-scale counterinsurgency wars in Iraq and Afghanistan must not negatively impact the integration of SOF-CIA operations or undermine the goals of seamless sharing of battlefield intelligence and close coordination procedures.
- The time is ripe to take action on the discussions examining the overlap and ambiguities in the application of Title 10 and Title 50.[46]

None of these bulleted recommendations in and of themselves ensure a harmonious SOF-CIA collaboration. Much of the cooperation depends on the personalities—at the top and at the bottom—involved in making plans, deciding issues, and executing operations. Thus, it behooves each department to emphasize cooperation when appointing liaisons. Every Eden has its serpent, and the snake in Washington often takes the form of turf and budget rivalries tempting the bureaucracies to enlarge their bite of the apple for more funds or bigger scope. Admiral Olson expressed concern about the tightening budget picture and its impact on the special soldier-spy interaction. Borrowing an analogy from biology, he said: "Organisms tend to shrink so as protect their core."[47] A defensive posture might lead to strained relations between the two security agencies. Ways have to be found, according to the former Navy SEAL, to overcome any recurrence in tensions among the security services.[48]

Some Observations

Past performance is merely an indicator of possible future actions. If the recent past SOF-CIA interactions are an accurate forecast, then the special operator–spy relationship would appear to be on a smooth path. Nothing should be taken for granted, however. Another signpost indicating the Pentagon's desire for its own exclusive military intelligence service working with SOF arose during the Obama administration. In late 2012, the Defense Department unveiled a project aimed at transforming the Defense Intelligence Agency by adding undercover operatives to attain a level of sixteen hundred around the world within a newly established Defense Clandestine Service. At the time of the announced plans, the DIA had about five hundred case officers. Plans called for Defense Clandestine Service officers to get their assignments from the Pentagon and to work often with the U.S. Joint Special Operations Command. The additional DIA operatives were to take up intelligence-gathering priorities that the CIA was unable or unwilling to conduct, particularly in the area of battlefield information. Elite commandos, for example, might need the precise location of a surface-to-air missile site or the specifics on the number of militants and arms within a target. In a sense this differing view of intelligence needs, in fact, represented another rendition of the "knob-turners versus the door-kickers" perspective on roles and missions to combat terrorism.[49]

Three years after announcing its intentions, the Pentagon decided to scale back its plans to form an overseas spy service that would have competed with the CIA. Instead of training and deploying about a thousand classified case officers overseas, the Defense Intelligence Agency settled on half that figure. The cutbacks resulted, in part, from congressional opposition to the DIA plan over the lack of "details necessary for effective review and implementation."[50] The desire of the Pentagon to have its own spy force for special mission units, however, indicates that the CIA-SOF feuds may not yet belong to history.

The conclusion reached in this account notes a functioning integration between the two communities despite occasional frictions among participants. No major, let alone catastrophic, failure resulted from a breakdown in cooperation akin to the bureaucratic clash that enabled the 9/11 hijackers to sneak into the United States and dwell among its citizens for months in advance of their terrorism. The natural affinity between the two communities has, if anything, been strengthened since the World Trade Center collapsed into debris and dust. The campaign on Islamist terror, or euphemistically the fight against violent extremism, created a symbiotic interaction that evidenced no serious public dissensions between the two premier security agencies. In some specific cases, SOF-CIA operations have merged into one another as ultraviolet and infrared blend at the center of the light spectrum.

The blurring of the operational lines between SOF and CIA took place haphazardly and evolutionarily, not through specific legislation or hierarchical fiat. Such an ad hoc design, thus, has been tested by time and real-world experiences and practices.

Yet, circumstances will change. It may be time for discussions to take place that lead to the examination of the two overarching authorities that have governed the military and intelligence communities—Title 10 and Title 50. The best practices of the past decade might be codified so that they will not be undone just as haphazardly as they took place. One must be aware of reading SOF-CIA history backward: to regard their working in close tandem as proof of this inevitability. There was nothing in the stars or in destiny to guarantee this outcome. Up until recently, the American way of war was a vessel that contained relics of the past and seeds of the future. The emergent special force–spy fusion, it should be remembered, resembles a hologram. Look at it one way, and you see two collaborators working together for now. Hold it another way, and what becomes visible are two separate entities buffeted by different political, budgetary, and cultural winds that could divide the two communities.

Insurgent-based terrorism lurks menacingly on the horizon. The jihadi threat, indeed, is seeping into new areas, taking advantage of failing or failed states that cannot police their own ungoverned spaces. Jihadi movements have filled the political vacuum and have taken up arms against secular rulers or impious regimes in the Middle East and North Africa, such as Bashar al-Assad in Syria, Muammar Qaddafi in Libya, and Ali Abdullah Saleh in Yemen. The war against jihadi terrorism appears to be both intergenerational and indecisive unless America recognizes the metastasizing threat and wages a more determined fight.

The political pressure mounting against the CIA drone program could change, remove, or reduce the Agency from participation in the current U.S. counterterrorism strategy. As noted earlier, traditionalists favor a return to the Agency's gathering and analysis functions over its more recent emphasis on paramilitary tactics. The White House's own President's Intelligence

Advisory Board issued a classified report in early 2013 warning that the nation's spy agencies were paying inadequate attention to China, the Middle East, and other national security flashpoints. According to media news reports, the board's study blamed the Central Intelligence Agency's focus on military operations and drone strikes.[51] Soon after his U.S. Senate confirmation hearings, CIA director Brennan voiced hopes of returning the Agency to its traditional role of intelligence collection and evaluation.[52] Such an eventuality may see SOF or even the U.S. Air Force take over the drone operations for countries such as Yemen and Pakistan. As noted above, JSOC has already taken over the primary role in commanding the use of drones in the Iraq-Syria theater against the Islamic State. This role and its coordination of raid forces into Somalia, Syria, Libya, and Iraq brought JSOC some of the same unwelcomed media coverage that normally plagued the CIA.[53]

Nothing on the political or geographical horizon suggests a diminution of the dangers posed by Islamist armed groups in far-distant lands, who will not hesitate to strike within Western Europe and the United States. The roots of the Islamist terrorist threat are immense. Terrorism is wrapped up in the intractable crisis of militant ideology, poverty, lawlessness, injustice, and bad government. The result is a generational crisis. Indeed, al Qaeda, the inspiration of so much jihadi violence, realized the benefits of revising Clausewitz's famous dictum. Terrorism is now the continuation of politics. The Islamists' goal is the restoration of a medieval caliphate that fell in Turkey at the end of World War I. The jihadis' violence is directed at a new Islamicized millennium.

Speaking at the NATO summit in Newport, Wales, in early September 2014, President Obama pledged that "we are going to degrade and ultimately defeat ISIL, the same way we have gone after al Qaeda."[54] There and elsewhere, the president outlined a strategy of air strikes, the training of indigenous forces, and special warfare tactics. If the United States adheres to that strategy, then the SOF-CIA model sketched in this work will form the basis for many of its counterterrorism efforts against the proliferating scourge of political Islam.

The intelligence-driven strike campaign buys time while specially trained forces and other instruments of national power can be employed to set up indigenous defenses within beleaguered states under threat from Islamist terrorism. Even then, iron sharpens iron, and the Sunni jihadists will prove inventive, as they have been with green-on-blue attacks (military speak for host-nation soldiers killing their U.S. trainers and mentors), to eat away at the camaraderie and cooperation between SOF advisers and host-nation combatants. The Islamic State has already proved itself inventive by its surprising mid-2014 advance into northern and western Iraq. Fighting as forces approximating a conventional army, the Sunni-dominated Islamic State crushed and routed the U.S.-trained and U.S.-equipped regular Iraqi armed forces. It stunned not only Shiite-ruled Baghdad but also the Pentagon for its rapid advance and seizure of U.S. tanks and artillery, which it soon used against Iraqi and Kurdish defenders. The Islamic State, as it later dubbed itself, demonstrated that America's terrorist foes can be adaptive as well as formidable.

America's current counterterrorism strategy derives, in part, from Washington's reluctance to embrace a larger, more expensive game plan. Training local forces to fight Islamist networks spares the lives of American troops while indirectly engaging terrorist elements. Targeted killings through SOF-CIA collaboration contributes to keeping the terrorist leadership off balance, but it falls short of eliminating the jihadi threat. Thus, the fungibility of spies and soldiers, for now, will continue as they each toggle between the two national security roles. The current U.S. administration hopes to steer its response between the Scylla of large-scale ground wars and the Charybdis of terrorist attacks hitting home by neglecting to adequately combat jihadi movements far from the United States. The SOF-CIA weapon can hold terrorism at bay until the unlikely prospect that the Islamist fervor burns itself out before an unforeseen catastrophic event takes place. Or the United States and its allies can resolve to win the war on terrorism. An intelligence-driven specialized counterterrorism instrument honed by more than a decade of effectiveness offers an active defense for the United States until a new day arrives.

Notes

1. America's Early Unconventional Ventures

1. Eric Schmitt and Thom Shanker, *Counterstrike: The Untold Story of America's Secret Campaign against Al Qaeda* (New York: Times Books, 2011), 259.

2. Christopher Andrew, *For the President's Eyes Only: Secret Intelligence and the American Presidency from Washington to Bush* (New York: HarperCollins, 1995), 7.

3. Ibid., 11.

4. Alan Axelrod, *The War between the Spies* (New York: Atlantic Monthly Press, 1992), xi.

5. Jeffrey M. Dorwart, *The Office of Naval Intelligence* (Annapolis, MD: Naval Institute Press, 1979), 30–35.

6. Jules Witcover, *Sabotage at Black Tom: Imperial Germany's Secret War in America, 1914–1917* (Chapel Hill, NC: Algonquin Books, 1989), 63–66.

7. Henry L. Stimson and McGeorge Bundy, *On Active Service in Peace and War* (New York: Harper and Brothers, 1947), 201.

8. Thomas H. Buckley, *The United States and the Washington Conference, 1921–1922* (Knoxville: University of Tennessee Press, 1970), 176.

9. Mark M. Lowenthal, *Intelligence: From Secrets to Policy*, 5th ed. (Los Angeles: Sage, 2012), 18–19.

10. Brian McAllistar Linn, *The Philippine War, 1899–1902* (Lawrence: University of Kansas Press), 2000, 322–28.

11. U.S. Marine Corps, *Small Wars Manual* (Washington, DC: U.S. Government Printing Office, 1940).

2. World War II and After: The Catalysts for Cloak and Dagger

1. Tony Geraghty, *The Irish War: The Hidden Conflict between the IRA and British Intelligence* (Baltimore: Johns Hopkins University Press, 1998), 347.

2. Anthony J. Jordan, *Churchill: A Founder of Modern Ireland* (London: Westport Books, 1995), 70–76.

3. For an analysis of why the British prevailed in the Northern Ireland insurgency, see Thomas H. Henriksen, *What Really Happened in Northern Ireland's Counterinsurgency: Revision and Revelation* (Hurlburt, FL: JSOU Press, 2008).

4. Tony Geraghty, *Black Ops: The Rise of Special Forces in the C.I.A., the S.A.S. and the Mossad* (New York: Pegasus Book, 2010), xxiii.

5. One of the most comprehensive books on the SOE is William Mackenzie's *The Secret History of the SOE: The Special Operations Executive, 1940–1945* (London: St Ermin's Press, 2000).

6. E. H. Cookridge, *Inside SOE: The Story of Special Operations in Western Europe, 1940–1945* (London: Arthur Barker, 1966), 3.

7. The most fascinating account of this Anglo-American interchange is detailed in William Stevenson, *A Man Called Intrepid* (New York: Ballantine Books, 1976).

8. Ibid., 435–38.

9. Douglas Waller, *Wild Bill Donovan* (New York: Free Press, 2012), 23.

10. Alfred H. Paddock Jr., *U.S. Army Special Warfare: Its Origins*, rev. ed. (Lawrence: University of Kansas Press, 2002), 2–3, 152.

11. Ibid., 25.

12. For an excellent study of the Jedburgh teams, see Will Irwin, *The Jedburghs: The Secret History of the Allied Special Forces, France 1944* (New York: Public Affairs, 2005).

13. Amy B. Zegart, *Flawed by Design: The Evolution of the CIA, JCS, and NSC* (Stanford, CA: Stanford University Press, 1999), 175.

14. Paddock, *U.S. Army Special Warfare*, 28–29, 35.

15. Ibid., 35.

16. Winston S. Churchill, *The Closing of the Ring* (Boston: Houghton Mifflin, 1953), 408–503.

17. For the CIA antecedents in the OSS, see Mark M. Lowenthal, *Intelligence: From Secrets to Policy*, 5th ed. (Los Angeles: Sage, 2012), 19.

18. Thomas K. Adams, *US Special Operations Forces in Action: The Challenge of Unconventional Warfare* (London: Frank Cass, 1998), 44.

19. Zegart, *Flawed by Design*, 189.

20. Jeffrey T. Richelson, *The U.S. Intelligence Community*, 3rd ed. (Boulder, CO: Westview Press, 1995), 12–16.

21. Paddock, *U.S. Army Special Warfare*, 95.

22. Ed Evanhoe, *Darkmoon: Eighth Army Special Operations in the Korean War* (Annapolis, MD: Naval Institute Press, 1995), 154–60.

23. Paddock, *U.S Army Special Warfare*, 119–23.

24. Ibid., 129.

25. Ibid., 136.

26. Samuel A. Southworth and Stephen Tanner, *U.S. Special Forces* (New York: Da Capo Press, 2002), 19.

27. Adams, *US Special Operations Forces in Action*, 113, 119, 135; and John Marchinko, *Rogue Warrior* (New York: Pocket Books, 1992), 223, 232.

3. Specialized Soldiering and Intelligence Operatives in the Vietnam War

1. *U.S. Army/Marine Corps Counterinsurgency Field Manual 3-24* (Chicago: University of Chicago Press, 2007), 173–75, 190, 209.

2. Thomas K. Adams, *US Special Operations in Action: The Challenge of Unconventional Warfare* (London: Frank Cass, 1998), 68–69.

3. Douglas Blaufarb, *The Counterinsurgency Era: U.S. Doctrine and Performance: 1950 to the Present* (New York: Free Press, 1977), 138–45.

4. T. X. Hammes, "The Future of Counterinsurgency," *Orbis* (Fall 2012): 575.

5. Tom Clancy, *Shadow Warriors: Inside the Special Forces* (New York: Berkley Books, 2002), 162.

6. Christopher K. Ives, *U.S. Special Forces and Counterinsurgency in Vietnam* (New York: Routledge, 2007), 21.

7. Francis J. Kelly, *U.S. Army Special Forces, 1961–1971* (Washington, DC: Department of the Army, 1973), 35, 37, 40–43.

8. Roger Hilsman, *To Move a Nation: The Politics of Foreign Policy in the Administration of John F. Kennedy* (New York: Doubleday, 1967), 436–39.

9. Thomas H. Henriksen, *WHAM: Winning Hearts and Minds in Afghanistan and Elsewhere* (MacDill Air Force Base, FL: JSOU Press, 2012), 25–27.

10. Blaufarb, *Counterinsurgency Era*, 106.

11. Cited in David Tucker and Christopher J. Lamb, *United States Special Operations Forces* (New York: Columbia University Press, 2007), 91.

12. William Colby, *Lost Victory: A Firsthand Account of America's Sixteen-Year Involvement in Vietnam* (Chicago: Contemporary Books, 1989), 163.

13. Andrew F. Krepinevich Jr., *The Army and Vietnam* (Baltimore: Johns Hopkins University Press, 1986), 71–72.

14. Colby, *Lost Victory*, 164.

15. Ives, *U.S. Special Forces and Counterinsurgency*, 21, 91.

16. Colby, *Lost Victory*, 165.

17. Mark Moyar, *Phoenix and the Birds of Prey: Counterinsurgency and Counterterrorism in Vietnam*, 2nd ed. (Lincoln: University of Nebraska Press, 2007), 127–29.

18. Colby, *Lost Victory*, 166.

19. Shelby L. Stanton, *Green Berets at War: U.S. Army Special Forces in Southeast Asia, 1956–1975* (Novato, CA: Presidio Press, 1985), 79–83.

20. Quoted in Evan Thomas, *The Very Best Men—Four Who Dared: The Early Years of the CIA* (New York: Simon and Schuster, 1996), 327.

21. John L. Plaster, *Secret Commandos: Behind Enemy Lines with the Elite Warriors of SOG* (New York: Simon and Shuster, 2004), 326–44.

22. Richard H. Shultz Jr., *The Secret War against Hanoi* (New York: HarperCollins, 1999), 43.

23. Ibid., 44.

24. Ibid., 54.

25. T. L. Bosiljevac, *SEALs: UDT/SEAL Operations in Vietnam* (Chicago: Ivy Books, 1990), 30–36.

26. Susan L. Marquis, *Unconventional Warfare: Rebuilding U.S. Special Operations Forces* (Washington, DC: Brookings Institution Press, 1997), 22.

27. Ibid., 20.

28. Clancy, *Shadow Warriors*, 200–204.

29. Shultz, *Secret War against Hanoi*, 291.

30. Ibid., 301–3.

31. Ibid., 276–77.

32. George J. Veith, *Black April: The Fall of South Vietnam, 1973–75* (New York: Encounter Books, 2012), 225–26, 309–10.

33. Bruce Herschensohn, *An American Amnesia: How the U.S. Congress Forced the Surrender of South Vietnam and Cambodia* (New York: Beaufort, 2010), 8–11, 32–34, 42–43.

34. For a graphic description of this interservice friction, see Clancy, *Shadow Warriors*, 206–11.

35. John T. Carney Jr. and Benjamin F. Schemmer, *No Room for Error: The Covert Operations of America's Special Tactics Units from Iran to Afghanistan* (New York: Ballantine Books, 2002), 21–23.

36. Charlie A. Beckwith, *Delta Force: The Army's Elite Counterterrorism Unit* (New York: Avon Books, 1983), 142–45.

37. Paul B. Ryan, *The Iranian Rescue Mission: Why It Failed* (Annapolis, MD: Naval Institute Press, 1985), 107–21.

38. Tim Weiner, *Legacy of Ashes* (New York: Anchor Books, 2008), 406.

39. Robert M. Gates, *From the Shadows: The Ultimate Insider's Story of Five Presidents and How They Won the Cold War* (New York: Simon and Schuster, 1996), 138–39.

40. Stansfield Turner, *Burn before Reading: Presidents, CIA Directors, and Secret Intelligence* (New York: Hyperion, 2005), 187–88.

41. *The 9/11 Commission Report: Final Report of the National Commission on Terrorist Attacks upon the United States* (New York: W. W. Norton, 2004), 88–93.

42. Beckwith, *Delta Force*, 222.

43. Alan Hoe, *The Quiet Professional: Major Richard J. Meadows of the U.S. Army Special Forces* (Lexington: University of Kentucky Press, 2011), 143, 145, 151.

44. Carney and Schemmer, *No Room for Error*, 86–87, 100.

45. Stanley McChrystal, *My Share of the Task: A Memoir* (New York: Penguin, 2013), 118.

4. The Emergence of a New Security Architecture

1. Michael Smith, *Killer Elite: The Inside Story of America's Most Secret Special Operations Team* (New York: St. Martin's Griffin, 2008), 56–68.

2. For a cogent summary of legislative action, see Amy Zegart, *Flawed by Design: The Evolution of the CIA, JCS, and NSC* (Stanford, CA: Stanford University Press, 1999), 140–42.

3. For the actual citation, see Section 167, Unified Combatant Command for Special Operations Forces, Chapter 6, Title 10, U.S. Code (accessed March 28, 2015), http://uscode.house.gov/download/pls/10C6.txt.

4. Michael R. Gordon and Bernard E. Trainor, *The Generals' War: The Inside Story of the Conflict in the Gulf* (Boston: Little, Brown, 1995), 241–42.

5. Ibid., 243.

6. Rick Atkinson, *Crusade: The Untold Story of the Persian Gulf War* (New York: Houghton Mifflin, 1993), 379–80.

7. Gordon and Trainor, *Generals' War*, 242.

8. Ibid., 243.

9. Mark Bowden, *Killing Pablo Escobar: The Hunt for the World's Greatest Outlaw* (New York: Penguin, 2001), 73–78.

10. Sean Naylor, *Relentless Strike: The Secret History of Joint Special Operations Command* (New York: St. Martin's Press, 2015), 57.

11. Mark Bowden, *Black Hawk Down: A Story of Modern War* (New York: Signet, 2000), 399–401.

12. William G. Boykin, *Never Surrender: A Soldier's Journey to the Crossroads of Faith and Freedom* (New York: Hachette Book Group, 2008), 281–92.

13. Richard T. Sale, *Clinton's Secret Wars: The Evolution of a Commander in Chief* (New York: St. Martin's Press, 2009), 332–43.

14. Naylor, *Relentless Strike*, 64–69.

15. Richard A. Clarke, *Against All Enemies: Inside America's War on Terror* (New York: Free Press, 2004), 224.

16. *The 9/11 Commission Report: Final Report of the National Commission on Terrorist Attacks upon the United States* (New York: W. W. Norton, 2004), 108, 134–37.

17. Quoted in Richard H. Shultz Jr., "Showstoppers: Nine Reasons We Never Sent Our Special Operations Forces after Al Qaeda before 9/11," *Weekly*

Standard, January 26, 2004, http://www.weeklystandard.com/Content/Public/Articles/000/000/003/613twavk.asp.

18. Daniel Benjamin and Steven Simon, *The Age of Sacred Terror* (New York: Random House, 2002), 294–96.

19. Shultz, "Showstoppers," 5.

20. Ibid.

21. Thomas H. Henriksen, *American Power after the Berlin Wall* (New York: Palgrave Macmillan, 2007), 52, 134.

22. Hy S. Rothstein, *Afghanistan and the Troubled Future of Unconventional Warfare* (Annapolis, MD: Naval Institute Press, 2006), 93.

5. September 11th and the Integration of Special Operators and Intelligence Officers

1. For a significant analysis, see Andru E. Wall, "Demystifying the Title 10–Title 50 Debate: Distinguishing Military Operations, Intelligence Activities, and Covert Action," *Harvard National Security Journal* 3 (2012): 101 (accessed March 22, 2015), http://harvardnsj.org/wp-content/uploads/2012/01/Vol.-3_Wall1.pdf.

2. Peter Bergen, *Manhunt* (New York: Broadway Books, 2013), 152.

3. Wall, "Demystifying the Title 10–Title 50 Debate," 92, 100, 107.

4. Mark Lowenthal, *Intelligence: From Secrets to Policy*, 5th ed. (Los Angeles: Sage, 2012), 192–94.

5. George Tenet, *At the Center of the Storm: My Years at the CIA* (New York: HarperCollins, 2007), 207.

6. Bob Woodward, *Bush at War* (New York: Simon and Schuster, 2002), 50–51.

7. Donald Rumsfeld, *Known and Unknown: A Memoir* (New York: Sentinel, 2011), 375.

8. Tenet, *At the Center of the Storm,* 175–84.

9. Sean Naylor, *Relentless Strike: The Secret History of Joint Special Operations Command* (New York: St. Martin's Press, 2015), 98.

10. Henry A. Crumpton, *The Art of Intelligence: Lessons from a Life in the CIA's Clandestine Service* (New York: Penguin Press, 2012), 225–26.

11. Woodward, *Bush at War,* 202.

12. Gary Berntsen, *Jawbreaker: The Attack on Bin Laden and Al-Qaeda: A Personal Account by CIA's Key Field Commander* (New York: Three Rivers Press, 2005), 75.

13. Rumsfeld, *Known and Unknown,* 375, 391–92.

14. Naylor, *Relentless Strike,* 125, 138–41.

15. Geoffrey Ingersoll, "The Most Elite Special Forces in the US," *Business Insider,* February 26, 2013 (accessed March 22, 2015), http://www.businessinsider.com/most-elite-special-forces-in-the-us-2013-2.

16. Douglas J. Feith, *War and Decision: Inside the Pentagon at the Dawn of the War on Terrorism* (New York: Harper, 2008), 112.

17. Naylor, *Relentless Strike*, 172–73.

18. Bergen, *Manhunt*, 152.

19. Dana Priest and William M. Arkin, *Top Secret America; The Rise of the New American Security State* (New York: Little, Brown, 2011), 236–37.

20. Gary Schroen, *First In: An Insider's Account of How the CIA Spearheaded the War on Terror in Afghanistan* (New York: Ballantine, 2005), 192, 197, 199. For an account that calls more attention to SOF/CIA bickering, see Eric Blehm, *The Only Thing Worth Dying For* (New York: Harper Perennial, 2010), 79.

21. Berntsen, *Jawbreaker*, 287.

22. Ibid.

23. Schroen, *First In*, 175, 192, 194–95, 270.

24. Ibid., 316–17, 347.

25. Naylor, *Relentless Strike*, 142–49.

26. Mir Bahmanyar, *Shadow Warriors: A History of the US Army Rangers* (New York: Osprey Publishing, 2005), 178.

27. Berntsen, *Jawbreaker*, 287.

28. Kathryn Stone, "All Necessary Means: Employing CIA Operatives in a Warfighting Role alongside Special Operations Forces," U.S. Army War College (accessed March 22, 2015), http://www.fas.org/irp/eprint/stone.pdf.

29. Dalton Fury, *Kill Bin Laden: A Delta Force Commander's Account of the Hunt for the World's Most Wanted Man* (New York: St. Martin's Press, 2008), 98, 105, 236.

30. Ibid., 278.

31. In his book, SEAL Team 10 petty officer Marcus Luttrell recounts that his four-man detachment received "very decent intel" targeting a mid-level anti-U.S. militia leader from the CIA for its late June 2005 assassination mission; see Luttrell, *Lone Survivor* (New York: Back Bay Books, 2007), 179–80.

32. Bob Woodward, *Obama's Wars* (New York: Simon and Schuster, 2010), 8, 355.

33. Ibid., 367.

34. Mark Mazzetti, *The Way of the Knife* (New York: Penguin Press, 2013), 206.

35. Greg Miller and Julie Tate, "CIA Shifts Focus to Killing Targets," *Washington Post*, September 1, 2011, A1.

36. Linda Robertson, *One Hundred Victories: Special Ops and the Future of American Warfare* (New York: Public Affairs, 2013), 198.

37. Ibid., 197.

38. Craig Whitlock and Greg Miller, "Paramilitary Forces Key for CIA," *Washington Post*, September 23, 2010, A1.

39. Rod Norland, "After Airstrike: Afghan Points to C.I.A. and Secret Militias," *New York Times*, April 10, 2013, A1.

40. David Jolly, "C.I.A.-Trained Forces in Afghanistan Scrutinized after Civilian Deaths," *New York Times*, December 4, 2015, A14.

41. Mark Mazzetti, Nicholas Kulish, Christopher Drew, Serge F. Kovaleski, Sean D. Naylor, and John Ismay, "The Secret History of SEAL Team 6: Quiet Killings and Blurred Lines," *New York Times*, June 6, 2015, A1.

42. Ibid., A14.

43. For an adequate summary of the AfPax Insider scheme, see Mazzetti, *Way of the Knife*, 197–211.

44. Ibid., 210–11.

45. Marc Ambinder, "Obama Gives Commanders Wide Berth for Secret Warfare," *Atlantic*, May 25, 2010 (accessed March 23, 2015), http://www .theatlantic.com/politics/archive/2010/05/obama-gives-commanders -wide-berth-for-secret-warfare/57202/.

46. Eric Schmitt and Thom Shanker, *Counterstrike: The Untold Story of America's Secret Campaign against Al Qaeda* (New York: Times Books, 2011), 245.

47. Mark Mazzetti, "U.S. Is Said to Expand Secret Actions in Mideast," *New York Times*, May 24, 2010, A1.

48. Mark Bowden, "Jihadists in Paradise," *Atlantic*, March 2007, 60.

49. Tony Geraghty, *Black Ops: The Rise of Special Forces in the C.I.A., the S.A.S. and the Mossad* (New York: Pegasus Books, 2010), 130.

50. Schmitt and Shanker, *Counterstrike*, 243.

51. Bergen, *Manhunt*, 120–21.

52. Rumsfeld, *Known and Unknown*, 464.

53. Ibid., 520.

54. Shane Harris, *@WAR: The Rise of the Military-Internet Complex* (Boston: Mariner Books, 2004), 19.

55. Ibid.

56. Ibid., 13–15.

57. Naylor, *Relentless Strike*, 229, 258–59.

58. Ibid., 294.

59. Tenet, *At the Center of the Storm*, 385–99.

60. Fred Kaplan, *The Insurgents: David Petraeus and the Plot to Change the American Way of War* (New York: Simon and Schuster, 2013), 304.

61. Priest and Arkin, *Top Secret America*, 242.

62. Stanley McChrystal, *My Share of the Task: A Memoir* (New York: Penguin, 2013), 117.

63. Ibid.

64. Priest and Arkin, *Top Secret America*, 235–37.

65. Harris, *@WAR*, 17.
66. Ibid.
67. McChrystal, *My Share of the Task*, 279.
68. Schmitt and Shanker, *Counterstrike*, 72.
69. Priest and Arkin, *Top Secret America*, 87.
70. Ibid.
71. Ibid., 227–28.
72. Mazzetti, *Way of the Knife*, 75.
73. Ibid., 149.
74. Lowenthal, *Intelligence: From Secrets to Policy*, 193.
75. *The 9/11 Commission Report: Final Report of the National Commission on Terrorist Attacks upon the United States* (New York: W. W. Norton, 2004), 415.
76. Mazzetti, *Way of the Knife*, 77.
77. Ibid.
78. Intelligence Authorization Act of 1991, Pub. L. No. 102–88, August 14, 1991 (accessed March 17, 2015), http://www.intelligence.senate.gov/laws/pl102-88.pdf.
79. Mazzetti, *Way of the Knife*, 80.
80. Rumsfeld, *Known and Unknown*, 391–92.
81. Geraghty, *Black Ops*, 134.
82. Mazzetti, *Way of the Knife*, 135, 269.

6. The SOF-CIA Fusion Concept in Two Theaters

1. Stanley McChrystal, *My Share of the Task: A Memoir* (New York: Penguin, 2013), 117.
2. Ibid.
3. Ibid., 118.
4. Ibid., 151.
5. Ibid., 152.
6. All quotes in the bulleted items are from McChrystal, *My Share of the Task*, 118.
7. Michael Weiss and Hassan Hassan, *ISIS: Inside the Army of Terror* (New York: Regan Arts, 2015), 27.
8. McChrystal, *My Share of the Task*, 149.
9. Ibid., 151, 157, 169.
10. Eric Schmitt and Thom Shanker, *Counterstrike: The Untold Story of America's Secret Campaign against Al Qaeda* (New York: Times Books, 2011), 164–65.
11. McChrystal, *My Share of the Task*, 23–32.

12. Ari Peritz and Eric Rosenbach, *Find, Fix, Finish: Inside the Counterterrorism Campaigns that Killed Bin Laden and Devastated al-Qaeda* (New York: Public Affairs, 2012), 128.

13. William Knarr, "Al-Sahawa: An Awakening in Al Qaim," *CTX Journal* (May 2013); Jim Michaels, *A Chance in Hell* (New York: St. Martin's Press, 2010), 64–103.

14. Bill Ardolino, *Fallujah Awakens: Marines, Sheikhs, and the Battle against al Qaeda* (Annapolis, MD: Naval Institute Press, 2013), 157–72.

15. McChrystal, *My Share of the Task*, 242.

16. Without revealing her identity, the task force commander alludes to "M.S.," a woman whose role "had been fundamental to the final stages of the Zarqawi hunt"; see ibid., 247.

17. Ibid., 256.

18. Michael R. Gordon and Bernard E. Trainor, *The Endgame: The Inside Story of the Struggle for Iraq, from George W. Bush to Barack Obama* (New York: Pantheon Books, 2012), 553.

19. Pamela Constable, "Mullen Visits Pakistan as U.S. Raids Stir Tensions," *Washington Post*, September 17, 2008, A13.

20. Richard Miniter, *Leading from Behind: The Reluctant President and the Advisors Who Decide for Him* (New York: St. Martin's Griffin, 2012), 140.

21. Eric Schmitt and Thom Shanker, "Officials Say U.S. Killed an Iraqi in Raid in Syria," *New York Times*, October 28, 2008, A1.

22. "Press Briefing by Bruce Riedel, Ambassador Richard Holbrooke, and Michelle Flournoy on the New Strategy for Afghanistan and Pakistan," March 27, 2009 (accessed March 22, 2015), http://www.whitehouse.gov/the_press_office/Press-Briefing-by-Bruce-Riedel-Ambassador-Richard-Holbrooke-and-Michelle-Flournoy-on-the-New-Strategy-for-Afghanistan-and-Pakistan.

23. Ibid.

24. Ibid.

25. McChrystal, *My Share of the Task*, 366–67.

26. Ibid., 380.

27. Peter Bergen, *Manhunt* (New York: Broadway Books, 2013), 92.

28. Karen De Young, "Brennan Reshaped Anti-Terror Strategy," *Washington Post*, October 25, 2012, A1; Yochi J. Dreazen, "Rolling Out Global Hit Teams," *National Journal*, September 3, 2011.

29. Bergen, *Manhunt*, 160.

30. McChrystal, *My Share of the Task*, 266.

31. Mark Owen, *No Easy Day* (New York: Dutton, 2012), 152.

32. Ibid., 183.

33. David E. Sanger, *Confront and Conceal: Obama's Secret Wars and Surprising Use of American Power* (New York: Crown Publishers, 2012), 79.

34. Bergen, *Manhunt*, 166–67.

35. For more information on the Panetta interview and the Title 10–Title 50 debate, see Andru E. Wall, "Demystifying the Title 10–Title 50 Debate: Distinguishing Military Operations, Intelligence Activities, and Covert Action," *Harvard National Security Journal* 3 (2012): 101 (accessed March 22, 2015), http://harvardnsj.org/wpcontent/uploads/2012/01/Vol.-3_Wall1.pdf.

36. Schmitt and Shanker, *Counterstrike*, 245.

37. McChrystal, *My Share of the Task*, 250.

38. Thomas H. Henriksen, *Afghanistan, Counterinsurgency and the Indirect Approach* (Hurlburt Field, FL: JSOU Press, 2010), 26–33.

39. Mark Mazzetti, "Efforts by CIA Fail in Somalia, Officials Charge," *New York Times*, August 11, 2006, A1.

7. SOF-CIA in Somalia, Yemen, and Beyond

1. Michael Weiss and Hassan Hassan, *ISIS: Inside the Army of Terror* (New York: Regan Arts, 2015), 114–30.

2. Michael Smith, *Killer Elite: The Inside Story of America's Most Secret Special Operations Team* (New York: St. Martin's Griffin, 2008), 237–38, 278–79.

3. Sean Naylor, *Relentless Strike: The Secret History of Joint Special Operations Command* (New York: St. Martin's Press, 2015), 326.

4. Mark Mazzetti, *The Way of the Knife* (New York: Penguin Press, 2013), 149–50.

5. Stanley McChrystal, *My Share of the Task: A Memoir* (New York: Penguin, 2013), 200.

6. Eric Schmitt and Jeffrey Gettleman, "Qaeda Leader Reported Killed in Somalia," *New York Times*, May 1, 2008, A7.

7. Jeffrey Gettleman and Eric Schmitt, "U.S. Kills Top Qaeda Leader in Southern Somalia," *New York Times*, September 15, 2009, A3.

8. Ty McCormick, "Exclusive: U.S. Operates Drones from Secret Bases in Somalia," *Foreign Policy*, July 2, 2015 (accessed December 20, 2015), http://foreignpolicy.com/2015/07/02/exclusive-u-s-operates-drones-from-secret-bases-in-somalia-special-operations-jsoc-black-hawk-down.

9. Daniel Klaidman, *Kill or Capture: The War on Terror and the Soul of the Obama Presidency* (New York: Houghton Mifflin Harcourt, 2012), 262.

10. Maria Abi-Habib, "Yemen Exposes Difficulties in U.S. Strategy," *Wall Street Journal*, December 4, 2014, A13.

11. Adam Entous, Julian E. Barnes, and Siobhan Gorman, "CIA Ramps Up Role in Iraq," *Wall Street Journal*, March 12, 2013, A1.

12. Ken Dilanian, "CIA, Special Ops Cooperate to Kill Extremists in Syria, Iraq," *Military Times*, September 28, 2015 (accessed December 20, 2015), http://www.military.com/daily-news/2015/09/28/cia-special-operations-cooperate-kill-extremists-in-syria-iraq.html.

13. John D. McKinnon, "Obama Faces Criticism for Declaring Islamic State 'Contained,'" *Wall Street Journal*, November 16, 2015, A8.

14. Tom Vanden Brook, "Special Operations Strike Force Heading to Iraq," *USA Today*, December 1, 2015, A1.

15. Ibid.

16. Helene Cooper and Eric Schmitt, "ISIS Official Killed in U.S. Raid in Syria, Pentagon Says," *New York Times*, May 16, 2015, A1.

17. Dana Priest and William M. Arkin, *Top Secret America; The Rise of the New American Security State* (New York: Little, Brown, 2011), 244, 253.

18. Eric Schmitt and Thom Shanker, *Counterstrike: The Untold Story of America's Secret Campaign against Al Qaeda* (New York: Times Books, 2011), 259.

19. Adam Entous and Siobhan Gorman, "U.S. to Expand Role in Africa," *Wall Street Journal*, January 29, 2013, A1.

20. Mark Mazzetti and Eric Schmitt, "Pentagon Seeks to Knit Foreign Bases into ISIS-Foiling Network," *New York Times*, December 11, 2015, A1.

21. Ibid.

22. Craig Whitlock and Greg Miller, "U.S. Official Says Al-Qaeda Could Fold in Two Years," *Washington Post*, September 14, 2011, A12.

23. For a particularly hard-hitting journalistic assessment, see "The Drone Papers," *Intercept* (accessed January 2, 2016), https://theintercept.com/drone-papers.

24. Greg Miller, "Secret Report Raises Alarms on Intelligence Blind Spots because of AQ Focus," *Washington Post*, March 20, 2013, A1.

25. Greg Miller, "Warning on Focus of Spy Agencies," *Washington Post*, March 24, 2013, A1.

26. Mark Mazzetti, "A Secret Deal on Drones, Sealed in Blood," *New York Times*, April 6, 2013, A1.

27. Jane Harman, "Drone Courts Can Work" *CNN Security Clearance—CNN.com* (accessed March 22, 2015), http://security.blogs.cnn.com/2013/02/19/harman-drone-courts-can-work/.

28. Mark Mazzetti, Charlie Savage, and Scott Shane, "How a U.S. Citizen Came to Be in America's Cross Hairs," *New York Times*, March 9, 2013, A1.

29. Mark Mazzetti and Eric Schmitt, "First Evidence of a Blunder in Drone Strike: 2 Extra Bodies," *New York Times*, April 23, 2015, A1.

30. Editorial, "A Debate on Strategy," *Washington Post*, January 9, 2013, A14.

31. William J. Daugherty, *Executive Secrets: Covert Action and the Presidency* (Lexington: University of Kentucky Press, 2004), 9–22.

32. Eric T. Olson, telephone interview by author, May 3, 2013. Admiral Olson was USSOCOM commander from 2007 to 2011.

33. Michael Hayden, interview by author, November 29, 2012, Washington, D.C. Hayden, U.S. Air Force general (retired), served as director of the

National Security Agency (1999–2005) and director of the Central Intelligence Agency (2006–9).

34. Olson, interview.

35. Ibid.

36. Greg Miller and Julie Tate, "CIA Shifts Focus to Killing Targets," *Washington Post*, September 1, 2011, A1.

37. Scott Shane, "Targeted Killing Comes to Define War on Terror," *New York Times*, April 8, 2013, A1.

38. Mazzetti, *Way of the Knife*, 299–321; Priest and Arkin, *Top Secret America*, 256–77.

39. Azmat Khan, "JSOC Using Captured Militants to Analyze Intel," *Frontline*, PBS, September 6, 2011 (accessed March 22, 2015), http://www. pbs.org/wgbh/pages/frontline/afghanistan-pakistan/jsoc-using-captured -militants-to-analyze-intel/.

40. Richard L. Russell, "Tug of War: The CIA's Uneasy Relationship with the Military," *SAIS Review* 22, no. 2 (Summer–Fall, 2002): 8.

41. Miller, "Secret Report Raises Alarms," A1.

42. Mark Mazzetti, "C.I.A. to Focus More on Spying, a Difficult Shift," *New York Times*, May 24, 2013, A1.

43. For another, earlier set of recommendations, see Kathryn Stone, "All Necessary Means: Employing CIA Operatives in a Warfighting Role alongside Special Operations Forces," U.S. Army War College, 23–24 (accessed March 22, 2015), http://www.fas.org/irp/eprint/stone.pdf.

44. Hayden, interview. He made this suggestion.

45. *The 9/11 Commission Report: Final Report of the National Commission on Terrorist Attacks upon the United States* (New York: W. W. Norton, 2004), 416.

46. For more on this point, see Stone, "All Necessary Means," 20.

47. Olson, interview. He made this suggestion.

48. Ibid.

49. Greg Miller, "DIA to Send Hundreds More Spies Overseas," *Washington Post*, December 1, 2012, A1.

50. Greg Miller, "Pentagon's Plans for a Spy Service to Rival CIA Have Been Pared Back," *Washington Post*, November 1, 2014, A1.

51. Miller, "Secret Report Raises Alarms," A1.

52. Scott Shane, "Rights Groups, in Letter to Obama, Question Legality of Drone Killings," *New York Times*, April 12, 2013, A6.

53. Wesley Morgan, "The Not-So-Secret History of the U.S. Military's Elite Joint Special Operations Command," *Washington Post*, December 16, 2015, A1.

54. Helene Cooper, "Obama Recruits 9 Allied Nations to Combat ISIS," *New York Times,* September 6, 2014, A1.

About the Author

Thomas H. Henriksen is a Senior Fellow at the Hoover Institution, where he focuses on American foreign policy, international political affairs, insurgencies, and counterterrorism. He has written or edited more than a dozen books and lengthy monographs. Besides this current volume, his most recent books include *America and the Rogue States* (Palgrave, 2012) and *American Power after the Berlin Wall* (Palgrave, 2007). He is a trustee of the George C. Marshall Foundation. During 1963–65, he served as a U.S. Army infantry officer. His other public service includes membership on the President's Commission on White House Fellowships and the U.S. Army Science Board, for which he received a Certificate of Appreciation for Patriotic Civilian Service from the Department of the Army.

Index